Jack Rogers

EXPECT A MIRACLE !

EXPECT A MIRACLE!

LET GOD HEAL YOUR HURTS AND MAKE YOUR DREAMS COME TRUE

DALE E. GALLOWAY

Tyndale House Publishers, Inc., Wheaton, Illinois

Names and incidents mentioned in this book
have been changed to protect the privacy of
the individuals involved.

First Printing, October 1982

Library of Congress Catalog Card Number 82-60249
ISBN 0-8423-0822-9, paper
Copyright © 1982 by Dale E. Galloway
All rights reserved
Printed in the United States of America

CONTENTS

1   Sentence of Death   7

2   The Birth of a New Dream   19

3   How to See a Dream Come True   33

4   Dare to Risk Failure to Gain Success   47

5   Why Be Overrun When You Can Overcome?   57

6   Walking Wounded   71

7   Rebuilding Self-Esteem   89

8   Bitter or Better—The Choice Is Yours!   107

9   Dove or Pigeon?   119

10   New Hope—A Reality!   139

11   Make Love Your Number One Aim   149

Postscript   155

O N E

SENTENCE OF DEATH

For I know the plans I have for you, says the Lord, plans for welfare and not for evil, to give you a future and a hope (Jer. 29:11, RSV).

On a cloudy day in the fall of 1969, I was sitting in a restaurant on Southeast Eighty-Second Street in Portland, Oregon, unaware of the catastrophe about to strike my life. Seated across the table from me was the girl I had fallen in love with as a freshman in college. We had married in the summer of 1957 and had struggled together to get me through college, seminary, and the beginning years of my pastoral ministry. Now the struggle for economic survival was over. At age thirty, I was enjoying the success of pastoring one of the larger churches of our denomination in the state of Oregon. The future had never look brighter.

Then it happened. The volcano of pent-up emotions erupted. My wife of twelve years angrily pointed her finger at me and said, "I do not love you. I have never loved you, and I'm going to divorce you." The sentence of death had been pronounced.

Nothing worse could have happened to me as a

minister brought up in a God-fearing, Bible-believing, conservative church and home. The collapse of my marriage meant that in the eyes of my church family I was a failure. A failure as a husband, a failure as a minister, and even a failure as a Christian.

A few months after my wife filed for divorce, took our two children, and left, I received a second sentence of death. I was in Kansas City, Missouri, for a speaking engagement. One of the very top officials of our denomination that both my grandfathers helped pioneer invited me to be a guest in his home. Our families had been friends for years. In fact, my father, who was a respected administrator over 135 churches in Ohio for more than thirty years, was probably influential in helping to get this man elected general superintendent.

Wanting to help, the superintendent said, "Dale, I'm really sorry about what has happened in your life." I knew that he deeply felt what he was saying. But then, without any understanding of where my feelings were, he said, "Let's face it. You're finished in the pastoral ministry. But I'll tell you what I'll do, I'll do my best to get you a teaching job in one of our colleges."

What our family friend thought to be a compassionate gesture was the sentence of death to me. From age fifteen, I had felt the call of God upon my life for pastoral ministry. All of my goals and dreams were focused on answering God's call upon my life to be pastor of a growing New Testament church. Much of my adolescence and all of my adult life had been spent preparing for and steadfastly fulfilling this call. My life had been characterized by a singleness of purpose. Now I was being told by the highest leader in our church, a man whom I honored and respected, that I was to forget being a pastor!

Many of you know what it is to live under the dark cloud of a sentence of death. Up until the time of my sentence I'd always loved life. Now for the first time my will to die was stronger than my will to live because everything I lived for was being taken from me.

Do you know what saved my life? Do you know what kept me going when I didn't feel like getting out of bed in the morning? What gave me hope when people around me said I was a washout? I got into the heart of the Bible and encountered Jesus in a fresh new way.

I saw him suffer and die on a cross for my sins. That means he died for my failings, my shortcomings, my mistakes. The truth is that whatever is wrong with me and whatever is wrong with you, he died on that cross to forgive and make right. Thank you, Jesus, for the forgiveness of all sin and freedom from all guilt and condemnation.

The truth found in Romans 8:1 has become my liberator from the dark prison of guilt: *There is therefore now no condemnation to them which are in Christ Jesus* (KJV).

Jesus died to liberate you from sin and guilt.

The Bible tells the most amazing true story about how Jesus was put to death and buried. He became the victim of the curse of sin and death. But that's not the end of the story. In fact, it's just the beginning. Because on the third day he rose from the dead. He is alive! Jesus is the victor over anything and everything that has ever defeated us.

No matter how your life has been broken apart or how excruciating your suffering is at this moment or how hopeless your situation seems, I can tell you that there is hope. Jesus Christ is alive and there is hope. How do I know? Because I have experienced new hope in my life. Everything that I lost has been given back to me many times over.

Because Jesus is alive, there is hope.
Because Jesus is alive, every day is Easter.

In 1975 my first book *Dream a New Dream* (later retitled *Rebuild Your Life*) told the story of how God put the broken pieces of my life back together. Since that time I have received scores of letters from people who were hurting and asking for help.

There are two truths of which I am absolutely convinced. The first truth is that no person is hopeless, and the second truth is that no situation is hopeless. Why do I believe this? Because Jesus is alive. I have personally experienced his resurrection power in my life. And I have witnessed his resurrection power at work again and again in the lives of people I know.

BECAUSE JESUS LIVES, NO PERSON IS HOPELESS

A mother called from a neighboring city and asked if I would go see her boy, Harold Walling, who was in the county hospital. As I walked into the room, my eyes fixed on a husky man handcuffed to a hospital bed and wearing a body cast from his waist down. Harold, as it turned out, had a long police record.

Actually, Harold was a nice guy except when he got drunk, which was often since he was an alcoholic. When he got drunk he showed a mean streak that led him into trouble. The reason he was in a body cast was that he had gotten drunk and into trouble and was running from the police when a policeman shot him in the leg.

Harold had been through every kind of rehabilitation program our court systems could offer. To every psychiatrist, counselor, and social worker who had treated him, he appeared to be a hopeless alcoholic bent on spending his life in prison.

Today, Harold has become one of the lay pastors in our church. He has become a trustworthy, responsible

citizen in the community, working at the same job
for many years now and earning many promotions. He is
married to a beautiful woman who gives him an extra
portion of love. They own their own home. Some five
years ago he was miraculously healed of alcoholism. It
has been my joy and privilege to watch the progressive
healing of my friend, Harold Walling, over these many
years.

How did all this happen? How was this man transformed from a menace to society to a pillar of society? He
let the Christ, the Son of the living God, work his
resurrection power in his life.

The other day I heard something that made me furious.
Someone was talking about another person I know.
He was saying that person was hopeless.

To my mind, the most profane word in the English
language is not a four-letter word but an eight-letter
word: *hopeless.* To say a person is hopeless, or a
situation is hopeless, is to deny the power of the risen
Christ. In Psalm 42:5 we read this statement of hope:
"*Hope in God*" (TLB).

David committed the sins of adultery, murder, and
deceit. But the Bible tells us that when he repented
and came clean with God, God forgave him, restored him,
and once again used his life in mighty ways. Whatever
you have done wrong, God wants to forgive you, restore
you, and use your life in a meaningful way. Believe it.

Next to my office as the Senior Pastor of New Hope
Community Church, is the office of a 6' 10" giant. His
name is Rich Kraljev. He is my closest friend and
fellow pastor in a successful ministry. But success has not
always been Rich's experience. As someone has said,
"Sometimes you have to fail before you are prepared to
succeed."

In 1972 Rich knew all about failure. A few years before
he had blown a basketball scholarship to St. Mary's
College in California and failed to graduate. All of his life

he had been plagued with failure in the area of communi-
cation. His family was from Yugoslavia. When they
came to the United States, they settled in a part of Los
Angeles that was a ghetto, so to speak, an enclave of
immigrants who spoke only their native language. At
three or four years of age, Rich moved with his parents
into a more anglicized neighborhood. Struggling to
learn to speak English, Rich developed a very serious
speech impediment, commonly called stuttering.

As Rich grew up, his stuttering, coupled with his
overgrown size, made him the target of many cruel
taunts. This destroyed his self-esteem and caused him to
withdraw into himself.

By 1972, Rich was working for Western Airlines loading
bags. He was burying his talents and spent most of
his time running from his failures, escaping into the
illusion world of drugs. At this point in his life, it wouldn't
have taken an expert to say, "What a waste—no hope
for him to amount to anything."

Then something happened that changed it all. Rich
met Jesus Christ, the hope of our world. This young man,
who had been looking in all the wrong places to find
meaning for his life, found Jesus through his recently
converted drug dealer. A few days after Rich committed
his life to Jesus Christ, his speech impediment
disappeared. I believe that this was a miracle sign of
the new life that Jesus was giving to this young man.

When Rich received Jesus Christ, he was without
a church family. His wife bought him a Bible, and he
began to study the Scripture intensely to feed his
newfound faith.

Isn't it interesting how God weaves his plan? At the
very same time that a young minister, Dale Galloway, was
being torn apart by divorce and needed new hope,
this young man, very much in the hippie culture, strung
out on drugs, and going nowhere with his life, started
to discover new hope. In God's plan and timing, these two

men from such different backgrounds would experience renewal and be brought together as fellow workers in a great team ministry of new hope.

Rich Kraljev is today a confident, competent, and compassionate minister that God uses in very unique and special ways. Rich has finished his college education. He preaches, teaches, and speaks fluently without any speech impediment. God uses him daily to give to others the same new hope that he has received.

God delights in making successes out of failures.

**BECAUSE JESUS IS ALIVE,
NO SITUATION IS HOPELESS**
What is it that seems so impossible in your life?

Is there a habit that binds you and defeats you?
Is there hurt that refuses to heal?
Is there a financial problem that is worrying you to death?
Is there a burden that seems unbearable?
Is there a problem that overwhelms you?
Is there an obstacle that looks like a great mountain?
Is there a child out of control?
Is there a broken relationship that refuses to mend?
Is there a dream that has been dashed to pieces?

What do you do when life is tumbling in on top of you? How can you react positively to negative situations? Start by understanding that no situation is hopeless, though admittedly from the human viewpoint it's easy to lose hope in the face of overwhelming circumstances.

Take the example of Donald and Kathy. Last New Year's Eve was the lowest point in their lives. Due to financial reverses they had just lost their dream home and were being evicted. Their hearts were broken. As we prayed together and shared communion together with Jesus, I encouraged them to trust the Lord and not give up hope. To believe that somehow, some way God in his power would bring them through this and out on top.

Yesterday, six months later, with a big sunshine smile on his face, Donald happily shared with me how Jesus had helped them to get back into a home of their own. The house that they have just moved into is much bigger and nicer than the first home. The contract terms are at an unbelievably low interest rate with a manageable balloon payment not due for five years. Any realtor looking at their situation would have called it impossible to get them into any kind of a home, let alone an attractive, spacious, far-above-average home.

Is there anything too hard for God?

Right now many of you face problems which seem impossible—mountains which seem insurmountable. Some of you find yourselves in situations where you have just about given up hope. You're caught in the web of negative thinking and your mind is saying over and over, "It's not going to get any better. Why try? It never works out for me anyway. Nothing good ever happens to me."

All their married life Abraham and Sarah had wished for and dreamed of having their own son. Every passing year of barrenness added to their disappointment. When Abraham reached the age of 100 and Sarah the ripe old age of ninety, having a child was not only removed from the realm of the probable, but it was impossible according to all scientific and medical laws.

So impossible had their dream of producing a child become, that when God himself announced that they were going to have a baby,

Sarah laughed silently. "A woman my age have a baby?" she scoffed to herself. "And with a husband as old as mine?"

*Then God said to Abraham, "Why did Sarah laugh? Why
did she say, 'Can an old woman like me have a baby?'
Is anything too hard for God? Next year, just as I told you,
I will certainly see to it that Sarah has a son"* (Gen. 18:12-14,
TLB).

The next year, unbelievable as it was, the impossible
became possible, the dream became reality, and Sarah
gave birth to their first son, Isaac.

Nothing is impossible with God.

No physical situation is hopeless. Consider Wayne and
Carol Seiffert's story. Four years ago when their son
Jeff was born, the doctor said not to expect him to live. In
the newborn baby's stomach there was a growth the
size of an orange. Not knowing what had caused it, and
not having much hope, in desperation the doctors
operated. They removed part of his intestine which had
died and had filled him with infection. Following
the operation, they told the parents again not to expect
the baby to live. God's people prayed for healing and
the baby miraculously survived.

Fourteen months later Wayne and Carol noticed that
Jeff was not growing as he should. His arms were all
twisted and bent. They took him back to the hospital,
where the doctors diagnosed rickets. This was followed
by months and months of testing and hospital visits.
Wayne and Carol got to the point where they were
physically, emotionally, and spiritually wrung out. At the
end of their rope they turned their son over to God.
They put his life and the healing of that life into the hands
of the Powerful One and told the Lord, "Lord, if it
means taking him to heaven to heal him, then we will
accept that. We just put him into your hands."

Medically things looked hopeless. But with God all
things are possible. Because Jesus is alive there is always
hope. God began to work his healing power through

the doctors. Finally they discovered what was wrong and started a positive treatment, still warning the parents not to expect normal growth or life span.

Today Jeff is growing three times faster than the normal child. He is quickly catching up with bigger children his age. If you ask Wayne and Carol about Jesus Christ, they'll tell you Jesus is alive and there is hope. Because he's alive, their little boy has been healed.

Larry was a CIA agent, one of the youngest in the intelligence service, and rising fast. Then it happened. He came down with testicular cancer in 1969. It had metastasized and spread to the lymphatic system, which means that malignancy had been released throughout the body. The prognosis at that time was that Larry had terminal cancer and had at the most two years to live.

Painful surgery was followed by two years of chemo-therapy. Larry's hair fell out. The feeling that people were turned off by his appearance worked havoc with his self-esteem.

While Larry was under the sentence of death from cancer and it seemed things couldn't get worse, his wife divorced him. To add insult to injury, the CIA, assured that he was going to die anyway and feeling he was of no further use to them, retired him from active service and placed him on permanent disability. Would you say that Larry's situation looked hopeless?

Yet Larry refused to give up hope. Why? Because he came to know the living Christ personally. Fourteen years later, Larry has a lovely Christian wife and teaches school. I wish you could see his full head of black hair and his radiant, happy smile.

Believe it.
Because Jesus is alive, no situation is hopeless.

I regularly receive letters, calls, and visits from people whose marriages have deteriorated into what appears to be a hopeless situation.

This past year at our church we were upset to see one of our couples separate. They had received Jesus Christ and joined the church the year before. It was a second marriage for both of them, and as is so often the case, the husband did not get along with the wife's children. It was a case of wounded persons continually hurting each other.

After Terry and Becky separated, Becky had a lot of resentment and hate, so much so that it looked as if any chance of reconciliation was impossible. Her negative feelings were so strong that it polarized her entire family, both her parents, and her children against Terry. And Terry by his own admission had an explosive temperament.

We in the church family who cared a great deal for Terry and Becky kept hoping and praying for a reconciliation. But as the weeks and months went by, it appeared that they were never going to get back together. Humanly, there seemed to be no hope.

For months we even lost contact with Becky. Then one night the phone rang and it was Becky. She wanted to come over and talk with me. At once she began to tell me how wrong she had been, how much she needed God's forgiveness and healing of resentment in her life. I knew that something miraculous was going to happen.

Becky again yielded control of her life to the living Christ. She confessed how wrong it was to have ill feelings and how much, with God's help, she needed to change from being negative about Terry to being positive. As we prayed, Jesus came and began a healing within Becky that was to be the beginning of healing her broken marriage. What a thrill it was to see this couple come back together and ask for and give forgiveness to each other.

How wonderful to see God heal their hurts and give them a fresh new start together, then to see them learning to disagree agreeably instead of tearing each other apart.

Just last Sunday I watched them leave the church

hand in hand. Anybody could tell by the way they looked at each other that they were in love. Yes, there is hope for an estranged marriage. Yes, love can come alive again. All because Jesus is alive.

On that first Easter morning, Jesus turned his defeat into victory. Death was turned into life, hell was turned into heaven, sin was turned into forgiveness, separation was turned into togetherness.

Because Jesus is alive, out of my hopelessness came the dream of New Hope. In chapters to come, I'm going to share with you that new hope. We are going to talk together about the healing of hurts and building of new dreams.

TWO
THE BIRTH OF A NEW DREAM

Where there is no vision, the people perish (Prov. 29:18, KJV).

EVERYONE NEEDS A DREAM

Without a dream a person is not fully turned on to living.
It is an all-inspiring dream that makes you want to
bounce out of bed in the morning, heightens all your
senses, and makes the creative juices in your mind flow.
Far better, I think, to live to age thirty with a dream
than to live to be 100 without a dream. Dreams lift us,
inspire us, put enthusiasm into our lives, and make
life truly fun to live.

There are so many things that a dream can do for us.
A dream can:

Lift you up out of self-pity.
Let you know that you are someone special.
Give you a challenge to reach beyond where you are now.
Cause you to develop your God-given potential and abilities
   to the fullest.

It has been both my personal experience and observation that a person possessed with a dream welcomes each day with excitement and positive expectation. An individual without a dream tends to drift through life without any purpose and is often bored. What a difference there is between having a beautiful dream and not having one!

THE CONCEPTION OF A DREAM

At a very early age a beautiful, inspiring dream came into my mind and crystallized. The dream was that I would build the biggest church in our denomination. How did a young boy ever receive, nurture, and commit his life to the fulfillment of an awesome dream like that one?

Throughout my growing-up years my father was a church administrator of a district in central Ohio. As was the custom in those days, traveling church leaders and missionaries coming to our city, Columbus, would stay in our guestroom. All of my boyhood summers were spent participating in whatever was happening at the church camp directly across the street from the district parsonage where we lived. God used all of those positive influences and experiences to create within me a fixed desire to really make my life count for him.

Years before the contemporary church growth movement with its marvelous helps, I believed that churches were supposed to grow. I can remember how upset I would become when year after year many of my dad's churches would report little or no gain in membership. In my boyhood idealism I could not comprehend why a church with Jesus Christ as its Lord would not grow. Another thing that bothered me was why our denomination had so many small churches (less than 100 members) and no really large churches (more than 1,000 members).

Oftentimes I would carry my discontent over the lack of church growth to the man I admired most, my dad. With a great deal of displeasure I would say, "Dad, this lack of church growth is terrible." Or, "Why don't your pastors build a great church of more than 1,000 members?" My wise old dad would just smile as if to say, "If you think it can be done, why don't you do it?"

It became my dream to break through the barriers and build a big church within the framework of our denomination. Exactly how old I was when the dream began to form and was crystallized I do not know. But by the time I was fifteen years of age, my commitment to the dream was unyielding. I knew that I would go to Olivet College in Illinois, then to the theological seminary in Kansas City. Upon graduation I would pioneer a brand-new local church in our denomination.

In June of 1963, upon graduation from seminary in Kansas City, I went back to my home city of Columbus with the assignment of beginning a new church in the suburb of Grove City. The day we moved to Grove City to begin, we had no members and no buildings, but I had a big dream.

How do you begin to make a church where there hasn't been a church? There are a variety of successful approaches to planting a new church. I founded and established a denominational church in Grove City by spending four years going door to door. You might call it the "double-knocking approach." Every time I knocked on another door, at the same time my knees automatically knocked. As scary as this double-knocking experience was, I learned so much from it about people and their hurts and needs. Soon I started preparing all my sermons to meet the needs people had in their lives. And when I started preaching need-meeting sermons, the school we were renting for church services began to fill up.

During my four years of establishing the Grove City

church, membership grew from zero to over 150 members. This made Grove City the pacesetter in church growth in our denomination in the state of Ohio during that time. However, within me was a growing discontent because I had a vision for something more. What I longed to see was not just addition to the church but New Testament multiplication. So I accepted a call to be the pastor of an old established church in Kansas. This proved to be a mismatch for both myself and the people. My new methods of outreach to the unchurched just did not match up with their strong feelings about maintaining the status quo. There I spent two of the most frustrating years of my life, wanting to see the church grow and reach the unchurched and yet unable to make anything happen.

By the fall of 1969 when I arrived to pastor the Central Church of our denomination in Portland, Oregon, I felt like a lion just let out of a cage. I was ready to tear up the woods. Central Church had averaged approximately 200 people in attendance for years. The reason I accepted the call was that I was impressed by the desire of the church's leadership to move ahead and do something to reach unchurched people.

The match-up between the new pastor and the lay leadership of the church was like the right-size glove being put on the hand. Happily I plunged into the challenge full steam ahead. The church responded beautifully, and our attendance doubled in that first year. I was excited. The people were excited. I had the good feeling that I was standing right on the brink of seeing my dream of building a great church become a reality.

THE DEATH OF A DREAM
Having only tunnel vision, I was blind to the warning signals of trouble at home. Unexpectedly, my unhappy

wife filed for divorce and popped my balloon. Did you
ever see a child's face when his first balloon popped? One
moment his face is all aglow because in his hands he
holds something awesome; then the balloon pops and he
stands there in bewilderment with nothing left but
a limp shred of rubber. In all too short a time, my dream,
which had been lifting me to new achievements all my
life, was gone.

Often in life there is the age-old struggle between hope
and despair. I'm acquainted very well with both. Has
your life been broken apart? Are you disappointed? Have
your dreams been destroyed?

It is easy to dream when you are on top of the pile.
But what about when you are under the pile? When
you're down and out, don't you need a dream even more?
After all, it is the dream that gives that lifting surge
to life. Yes, everybody needs a dream.

Sometimes a dream has to die before it can live.

THE BIRTH OF A NEW DREAM

To me there is nothing more monotonous than to
live without a dream. Without a lifting dream, life
becomes like a fishing reel with the drag on. It's
a drag to even get out of bed, let alone go through the
day.

I continued to pastor the Central Church through
the crisis of my family breakup and the rebuilding
of my life through a love-filled marriage to my wife,
Margi. That church had some really beautiful
Christian people in it. Those dear people, even
though they didn't understand what was going on,
stuck by us in Christlike love. Margi and I will
both always be grateful for their love and friendship.

After Margi and I had married in August of 1971,
I began to get restless. A lot of inner healing had

taken place within me, and the love Margi and I shared
was like the springtime alive and blooming in beauty.
Still I had an uneasiness because for the first time in my
life I didn't have a dream.

Unexplainably, except for love, the people at Central
Church had kept me as their pastor through both the
divorce and the remarriage, but my ability to lead them to
higher heights had been damaged beyond repair. I
could never be content to stay and just survive. It was
obvious that no door of any other denominational
church was open for me to pastor.

One day, as I was talking to God about all of this, I
relaxed in his presence and opened my mind to receive.
The Spirit of the Lord directed me to open the Bible
and read these words from the book of Isaiah as read by
Jesus in the synagogue in the launching of his own
ministry.

*The Spirit of the Lord is upon me; he has appointed me to
preach Good News to the poor; he has sent me to heal
the brokenhearted and to announce that captives shall be
released and the blind shall see, that the downtrodden
shall be freed from their oppressors, and that God
is ready to give blessings to all who come to him* (Luke
4:18, TLB).

In that holy moment, I believe God dropped the idea
for a new magnificent dream into my mind. To me
the Spirit of the Lord said, "Son, I'm not finished with
your life yet. I'm going to heal your brokenness and
give you a greater dream than you've ever had before. I'm
giving you a vision of how to heal the hurts and build
the dreams of thousands of people. Take my love to those
who are down, beaten, bruised, and bleeding. Tell
them that I love them and want to heal them."

Thus, the birth of the dream—New Hope, a church for
the unchurched thousands! A ministry that would

specialize in healing the hurts and building the dreams of thousands. New Hope would be a healing fellowship that would not care where people had come from but only where they were going. A caring fellowship where anyone and everyone could find love, acceptance, and forgiveness. At New Hope people would learn to refuse to let past failures hinder them from living and enjoying today for God's glory.

TESTING THE DREAM
In the spring of 1972 I tested my new dream. I asked myself some very basic questions:

1. Would this be a great thing for God? The answer: it would be tremendous.

2. Would it help a lot of people who were hurting? The answer: yes, it could bring help and healing to scores of people.

3. Would it bring the best out of me? Answer: yes, it would be the challenge of my life to build something great out of nothing.

4. Have my experiences in life prepared me to fulfill this dream? Answer: way back when I was beginning my first church by going door to door, I had an awakening that more people could be reached by a nondenominational church than a denominational one. All of my life had been a preparation for this dream.

5. Was this something that God was asking me personally to do? Answer: who would be better equipped to heal the hurts of broken people than one who had been broken and healed himself? Who could better lead a ministry of reaching unchurched people than a young man who felt he no longer belonged in the church of his birth?

I tested my dream by talking to mature and wise Christian friends. Reactions differed widely. Most of our friends within our denomination were negative to the idea, while friends from other Christian circles were quite positive and encouraging.

How would my own father respond? He had spent his lifetime helping to build a major denomination from a few fragmented churches. If there was ever a denominational man, it was my dad. He was extremely loyal to his church and often had a narrow viewpoint toward other groups. You might say his strength was also his weakness; it's a good thing to be loyal, but not a good thing to be exclusive in one's Christian viewpoint.

As I broke the news to my dad that I was going to leave the denomination and begin an independent church called New Hope Community Church, I did not know how he would react. But he immediately accepted my new dream and believed in it. Before he passed away I think he was even proud to tell his contemporary church leaders what his son was doing. I only wish he could have lived to see what has happened in the ministry of New Hope Community Church over the last ten years. On the other hand, I guess he probably does see it all happening from where he is.

THERE IS NO GAIN WITHOUT PAIN

One of the most difficult things that Margi and I have ever done was to resign our pastorate at Central. It was excruciatingly painful for both of us to leave the denomination of our birth. It had nurtured us, educated us, and been such an important part of our entire lives. Margi had also been a preacher's kid, had grown up at denominational church camps, and had gone to the denominational college at Nampa, Idaho. Some of the pain from leaving we were to feel for years to come.

How do you support yourself financially when you are starting an interdenominational church? I spent hours putting together a dream booklet in which I pictured and dramatized what I planned to do. In it, I thought out and wrote down one-year goals, five-year goals, ten-year goals, fifteen-year goals, and twenty-year goals. It was the neatest booklet you ever saw. So I thought anyway.

Armed with my booklet and a big dream, I selected twenty people I knew whom I thought might help support this beginning ministry. I made individual luncheon appointments with each of the twenty. We had fine lunches that I couldn't afford, and I passionately shared my vision taking them step by step through the booklet. Do you know how many financial supporters for my new dream I had when finished? Zero.

At this point I almost killed the dream before I got started. I was depending on these people. Without them I didn't have any source of support. How alone and beaten I felt. Have you ever shared a beautiful dream with others and been unable to get anyone to respond positively to it?

A few days later as I was reading my Bible and asking God for direction, the Lord reminded me of a scriptural teaching that I had heard and read from Oral Roberts: *"Make God your source."* The moment I started making God my source, looking to him to supply our needs, I stopped feeling defeated and started believing that God would take care of us.

If God be for us, who can be against us? (Rom. 8:31, KJV)

The first Sunday in July 1972, was our last Sunday at Central Church. After we said our good-byes, it would be a long time before we would receive another paycheck. Margi had resigned her teaching job to help me begin the new ministry. We had big needs in our life. We needed some people to help us get started pioneering this new dream. We needed some people to pastor.

Soon we would be out of funds and we needed a way to buy groceries and pay the mortgage and meet all the other financial demands that go with daily life. Boy, did we have needs. We were all alone, without jobs, and ineligible for unemployment compensation.

Margi and I together read these words in Luke 6:38 and we learned about seed-faith giving:

For if you give, you will get! Your gift will return to you in full and overflowing measure, pressed down, shaken together to make room for more, and running over. Whatever measure you use to give—large or small—will be used to measure what is given back to you (TLB).

We concluded that we had a big need and that we needed to sow our biggest seed ever. What did we have to give? We had a thousand-square-foot new honeymoon house that we'd lived in since our marriage eleven months before. During the stress of being criticized and misunderstood and the adjustments of a new marriage, we had found shelter and abundant love together in our home. We loved that little house.

Margi's father and mother had never had a house of their own. As her father had moved from church to church in Washington and Oregon, the family had always lived in a church parsonage. Some of them had been good and some of them not so good. But it meant a lot for Margi to have a home of her own. We had put in the yard and flowers and the shrubs with our own hard work. Except for our love and our faith, at this time in our life that little house represented all that we had.

There is no feast without a sacrifice.

I will always love Margi for her giving. After much struggle and pain, she decided to join me in giving our house as a seed to launch the dream. We sold the house and took our $6,000 equity and gave it to the miracle worker, Jesus.

Within a year of the time the money was all gone, enough seed-faith givers had joined us in this pioneering adventure to provide for our financial support. Besides this, God brought to us a new builder friend who got us into a brand-new house a little bit nicer than the one we gave up. He got us into this house the only way we could have gotten into a house—without any down payment. In years to come the provision of a bigger house would come from God in miraculous ways and give us a more beautiful home than we could ever imagine.

Give and you shall receive.
There is no gain without pain.
First you give, and then you receive.

So many people want good things to happen in their lives and yet they are unwilling to pay the price. The best things in life cost something. And the more worthwhile it is, the more it costs. The fulfilling of the dream of New Hope was to cost us blood and sweat and tears. But the blessings and the satisfaction of seeing a beautiful dream coming true is without price.

Pursuing the dream was to cost us the pain of being severed from the church of our birth. Our denomination was unequipped to deal with what had happened in my life, in that it had no place for me to go, no recovery program, and no redemption for one of its own sons and pioneer grandsons. The church reacted in the only way it was programmed to act. Once the officials knew of my dream to begin New Hope Community Church, they informed me that they were dropping me from the ministerial roll. Accepting their judgment and not wanting to be rejected any further, I simply wrote a courteous letter and asked for my name to be removed from the roll. For years I was to live with the sorrow

and emptiness of no longer belonging to a church
that I loved, but I can tell you that out of that kind of
pain has truly come gain.

There is no personal growth without some struggles.

**In every crisis of your life there is an opportunity for
something greater.**

LAUNCHING THE DREAM

With the launching of New Hope Community Church,
Margi and I set out to do something greater than we'd
ever done before. We began by renting a second-story
office space on Lake Road. We affectionately came
to call it "the upper room." We began holding a weekly
Bible study there. In the pioneer group came the
Schmidts, the Watsons, the Burtons, the Molts, and their
friends the Runds, who became our first converts.
From the beginning there was a very special fellowship
of daring, caring, and sharing life together. Soon we
began to plan for our first service.

Where can a new church begin? I had heard my friend,
Dr. Robert Schuller, talk about playing the possibility
game. So that's what I did; I played the possibility game.
I took a piece of paper and wrote down ten possibilities
of where we might begin our church. The places included
a drive-in theater, a mortuary, an office building, a school
building, a Seventh Day Adventist church, and so on. I
arranged the list in terms of my highest preference. I went
to all ten on the list and asked for permission to use
their facility. Not one gave me an immediate answer.
Two weeks later the manager of the Eighty-Second
Drive-In Theater called and said that it had never been
done before that he knew of, but if we would pay the
rent, we could use the facility on Sunday morning. It was
my number-one choice on the list.

What did the drive-in have that the other places didn't? It had a parking lot for 800 cars. There wasn't a church in the city that could park 800 cars. Besides that, with people sitting in their cars during the service, we would have unlimited seating. The thing we were to learn was that only two kinds of people would come to the drive-in for church. One would be the completely unchurched person who was so wounded or so skeptical they would not go into a conventional church. The other kind of person who would come would be a possibility thinker—someone who had vision and wanted to do something more for God to help people than was being done in the average church. In God's perfect plan this made an unbeatable combination to work with.

The Sunday we set for launching the dream of New Hope was October 14, 1972. We advertised, we prayed, and we prepared. The launching day came. With the mixed emotions of anticipation and fear of failure, Margi and I drove to the drive-in early Sunday morning. Our few fellow pioneers from the Bible study came early. They were there to greet whoever would come.

Minutes before the announced hour to begin, Margi and I stood behind the snack shack nervously talking and wondering how many would come. At the appointed hour we put the ladder up. I kiddingly tell people that I pushed Margi up the ladder and she pulled me up from behind. One thing for sure, she wasn't going to walk the 100 feet across that roof without me. On the other hand, there was no way I would have missed walking across that roof to begin a ministry of New Hope.

It was a humble beginning. We had a little forty-dollar mike and a 100-foot cord and a wobbly recorder that played poor quality organ music. To our delight about fifty people came in different sizes and makes of cars. Margi, the trouper that she is, sang and I preached and we got started. I suppose to most people looking on it didn't look like much, but to us it was everything. We were doing what God wanted us to do. And one of the great truths that I have discovered is this: *There are infinite possibilities in small beginnings.*

How ridiculous to begin a ministry in rainy Oregon in a drive-in theater! As anyone who lives in Portland can tell you, in the fall it rains. But believe it or not, for the first fourteen weeks of the drive-in ministry it never rained on us. In the years to come it wouldn't matter whether it rained or not. But in the beginning in order to get off to a good start, it was crucial that we have good weather. And every Sunday for fourteen weeks was sunny.

In the fourteenth week on a Saturday, the pioneer men of our new venture built a platform in the front of the snack shack. It had an overhead covering that ingeniously folded down during the week for the movies, but came into place on Sunday morning to provide shelter for a young pastor and his wife and anyone else who would be helping to lead the service. On that Saturday night, at the very moment the movie began at the drive-in, the work on the new platform shelter was completed. That Sunday morning as Margi sang and I preached on the new platform with the little shelter over our heads, it poured down rain. It was as if God said, "It's about time for a little rain, don't you think?" I'll always believe God was in charge of the weather and gave us his smile of approval by providing sunshine in which to launch a great ministry of hope.

My friend, you, too, can dream a new dream. No matter who you are, no matter what your age, no matter what has happened, you can dream a beautiful new dream. I dare you to join me in dreaming God's dream for your life.

THREE

HOW TO SEE A DREAM COME TRUE

You see things as they are, and you ask why? But I dream things that never were: and ask why not? George Bernard Shaw

Where would I be today if I had stayed in my shell, licked at my wounds, wallowed in self-pity, and been satisfied to live in the failure situation in which I'd found myself? I'm filled with thanksgiving to God who put the desire within me for something greater, who gave me the faith and courage to dream a new dream. This is the same thing that God wants to do for you. But you must step out of the shell of past failures and reach forward to new horizons. The time has come for you to do something.

The other day I was having lunch with a man who after eight years of struggle and hard work was losing his business through bankruptcy. With tears in his eyes he said, "What'll I do?"

I said, "Why not do something greater than you've ever done before."

I have observed that most of the time people have to experience some failure before they are prepared to succeed. There is a world of difference, my friend, between failing and being a failure. Because you failed at a job does not mean that you are a failure. It simply means that you need to rise up and try something different. God didn't create you, me, or anyone else to be a failure. I love these words of Edward Hickson, "If at first you don't succeed, try, try again." In my opinion, anyone who keeps trying is never a failure.

God is in the business of helping losers to become winners. The world has a way of dividing people into two groups, winners and losers. Cynics believe that most people are losers, but God looks at every person and says, "*I created you to be a winner.*"

Did you ever see a bird flying against strong downward drafts and going nowhere? Now, birds were made to fly. To soar to the heights. But sometimes when a windstorm comes, the going gets tough.

My friend, the same God that made the birds to fly the heights made you to dream beautiful dreams and to make those dreams come true. In Jeremiah 29:11, I read about God's dream for your life in these words:

For I know the plans I have for you, says the Lord. They are plans for good and not for evil, to give you a future and a hope (TLB).

It is the difficult times of testing that prepare us to succeed. The most successful people I have ever known have all gone through their particular school of hard knocks.

In the Bible we read about a man who went through some rather difficult times of preparation before he succeeded. Having endured the unjust treatment that this man faced, many people would become bitter. Facing the hardships this man faced, most people would have given up their dream. But not Joseph. Joseph was not a quitter.

Joseph, the favorite son of Jacob, knew how to dream

big dreams. As a boy, many of his days were spent
tending his father's flocks and dreaming. Daily he fellow-
shiped with God and dreamed his beautiful dreams.
In his enthusiasm he would share with his brothers his
dreams of how God was going to use his life in a special
way.

Being negative thinkers, Joseph's brother branded
his dreams as foolishness. Worse yet, out of their own
insecurities, they let the green-eyed monster of jealousy
seize possession of their minds. When they could no
longer stand to hear their father and neighbors sing the
praises of Joseph, they formed a conspiracy to kill
their brother.

But at the last minute they changed their minds and
sold him into slavery instead, thinking they would
be rid of this dreamer forever.

Adverse circumstances cause many people to give up
on their dreams, to lose perspective on their overall
purposes and higher goals in living. Why should we
ever settle for less than the best? Joseph was one person
who refused to settle for less.

Sold into slavery, falsely accused in Egypt by a wicked
woman, and thrown into prison, Joseph stubbornly
refused to give up his dream. In his difficult times, he
drew nearer to God and kept believing that somehow,
some way, his impossible dream would come true.

In prison, instead of wallowing in self-pity, he
continued faithful to God and prepared to fulfill the
dream that God had given to him. And when, in God's
timing, the moment came that God wanted to use
him to lead the nation out of famine, Joseph was ready.

Did you know that things that are happening to
you right now are to prepare you to fulfill a beautiful
dream that God wants to place in your life?

I know it's tough when you are going through the time
of preparation. But if you learn your lesson well, and
you keep preparing, it's all going to be used to fulfill the

most beautiful dreams in your life. Believe me, I know what I am talking about.

Not many weeks after I dared to dream a new dream in my life, into my mind came a formula for fulfilling that beautiful dream. I call it the "Achiever's Creed." It has played a big part in making my dreams come true.

Whatever the mind can conceive
And I will dare to believe
With God's help I can achieve.

How do you fulfill a beautiful dream in your life? First, you conceive it. Second, you believe it. And third, you achieve it.

I. CONCEIVE IT

You have within your own brain the fantastic power to conceive a beautiful dream and pursue that dream to its fulfillment. Nothing in the universe can compare with the wonder of your own brain. No computer exists that can duplicate the functions and powers of your mind.

The shame is that most of us do not even begin to use one-tenth of our God-given brain's ability to conceive dreams. There is a whole world out there for our minds to explore.

The other day on television I heard a report of some of the things scientists are doing with laser beams. The reporter doing the commentary was predicting that in four or five years we would be using laser beams as weapons launched from outer space. When I heard that I thought: *Yes, what we read in science fiction and think is way-out, scientists make a reality ten or fifteen years later.*

Your brain is your marvelous gift from God.
How much you use it is your choice.

FIVE STEPS TO CONCEIVING AN INSPIRING DREAM
Step One—Fantasize. We are all born with a God-given
imagination. I remember as a child imagining all kinds of
fun-filled fantasies. In the world of play and make-
believe, there was no limit to what I could be and what I
could do.

We were not given imagination merely to use in
childhood and then put on the shelf for adulthood. What
has happened to that imagination we all had as children?
Imagination is like a muscle: you use it or you lose
it. And the more you use it, the more it comes alive.

This past July at our annual New Hope Family Camp
on the scenic coast of Oregon, I was given the assignment
of leading a class in dreaming. What an enjoyable
experience it proved to be. Each morning after breakfast,
our class would go to the beach together. There in
the awe-inspiring surroundings of sunshine, the vast
Pacific Ocean, and the endless sandy beach, we would
take our shoes off, sit down, and relax. I kiddingly told
the people they could dream better if they covered
their feet with sand. The truth is that you have to get your
head out of the sands of daily routine to explore the
vast possibilities of the exciting world of dreams.

Let your mind go. Ask yourself this question. If I could
do anything in this world that I wanted to do with
my life, what would it be? Now forget about everything
else and let your imagination dream. It doesn't cost
anything to dream. It's free and it's fun.

A beautiful idea is about to be dropped as a seed into your mind.

Step Two—Conceptualize. What at first appears impossible *is* possible. A lot of people are accomplishing
impossible dreams. Why not you?

My friend, there are so many wonderful things that can
happen to you if you will open your mind to receive

choice ideas that God has for you. I believe that all beautiful, worthwhile ideas come from God. And because God is no respecter of persons, he drops worthwhile ideas into the mind of everyone.

I remember a story that I've heard Dr. Robert Schuller tell about a strange fisherman. It seems that two fishermen are out in separate boats fishing. The one fellow, every time he catches a big fish, throws it back in. If you think that's strange, every time he catches a little one, he puts it on his stringer and keeps it. This goes on all afternoon.

The fisherman in the opposite boat has been watching the strange fisherman and just can't believe what his eyes are seeing. Finally his curiosity gets the best of him and he yells, "How come you keep throwing the big fish back and keeping the little ones?" The strange fisherman reaches down under the boat seat, pulls out his little frying pan, holds it up, and yells back, "Only the little fish will fit in my frying pan."

How we laugh at the strange fisherman. Yet isn't this exactly what we do? We keep the little ideas and throw out the big ones. We think the big ones are impossible so we throw them out. What we need to realize is that the big dreams are not any more impossible to fulfill than little dreams. The difference between little dreams and big dreams is that big dreams take a longer time to come true.

I believe in big dreams. Big, beautiful, *risky* dreams come from God. God's biggest dreams for your life are humanly impossible to fulfill. To see the big dreams through, you are going to have to depend on your heavenly Father. And besides that, you're going to need a lot of other people to help you fulfill that dream. It has been my experience that big dreams attract other people's help. Whatever you do, don't torpedo your dream by saying it's impossible. Open your mind to explore all the potential and possibility of the idea that has come into your mind. *Every beautiful, inspiring dream begins with a God-given idea planted as a seed in a receptive mind.*

Step Three—Scrutinize. Ask yourself every question you can think of concerning this idea: Would this be a great thing for God? Would this help other people? Is anybody else doing this? Would this bring the best out in me? Have I been prepared to do this?

Seek knowledge. Gather all the facts and figures you can. Find out if there is an untapped market for your idea.

Seek advice. Talk to experts. It is amazing how many experts will give you hours of free advice if you will seek them out and listen. People love to talk about their area of special knowledge. Every good idea will stand up to complete examination. If you are afraid to discuss your idea, your dream, with friends and experts, the chances are you are playing games with yourself. Deep inside you may already know the idea is not a worthwhile one.

But don't expect all your friends to respond positively to your dream. If I had listened to the people who surrounded me and whom I first talked to about the dream of New Hope, the newborn dream would have died in the incubator. There is something wrong with every worthwhile idea. Just because there is something wrong with it need not keep it from becoming your greatest dream.

Step Four—Crystallize It. Focus in on your dream and see if you can put it in a capsule form. My dream of New Hope in capsule form was to build a church for the unchurched, the purpose of which was to heal the hurts and build the dreams of thousands.

In this stage of developing your dream, set down on paper your objectives and purposes. I wrote on a sheet of paper the objectives and purposes of New Hope

Community Church. Later these objectives and purposes
were accepted and adopted by the New Hope
Community Church Session (this is our governing board
of directors). In the days and years that followed,
these objectives kept us on target in achieving the dream
of New Hope.

Here are our eight objectives and purposes:

1. *Reach unchurched thousands.*
2. *Healing center.*
3. *Edifying center.*
4. *Equipping center.*
5. *Build strong Christian families.*
6. *Christ center of positive inspiration.*
7. *Deploying center.*
8. *Worship center.*

There are many ministries we could do as a church,
but we select the ministries which best carry out the
objectives and purposes we have crystallized.

Crystallizing your dream means drawing the plans for
how it is to be accomplished. Dreams don't just
happen. There are a lot of people who dream beautiful
dreams, but that's the end of it.

To succeed you must plan to succeed. As someone
has said, "To fail to plan is to plan to fail." Draw your plan
step by step. You've got to be selective. You can't fulfill
a big dream all at once.

Many small businesses and churches are failing simply
because they're trying to do more than they are capable of
doing. Trying to do many things, they end up doing
nothing well. What they need is to pick out what they can
do best and do that only. Get the success momentum
going; then add additional services.

For example, in developing the dream of New Hope
Community Church, it was several years before we had a
Christian education program. Not because we didn't

believe in Christian education, but because we were not equipped or ready to do a successful job in this area. The strongest thing we had to begin with was my own gifts and abilities to preach need-meeting, positive sermons. So, that's what we majored on. But that is something we planned.

Crystallize your dream by setting long-range goals, medium-range goals, and short-range goals. Previous to launching my dream of New Hope, I sat down and wrote on paper what I thought were giant goals for twenty years, fifteen years, ten years, five years and each year leading up to the fifth year in the areas of member-ship, attendance, finances, and need-meeting ministries. For example, my ten-year goal for membership was to have 1,000 members. As I write this, months before our tenth-anniversary celebration, we already have 1,300 members. And thank you, Jesus, because all my other ten-year goals are fulfilled. Amazingly some of the fifteen-year goals are also fulfilled. Incredible things happen when we take the time to plan and to set goals for them to happen.

The more time you spend in planning, the better prepared you are to succeed.

Step Five—Visualize. The finest cameras do not have the astounding picture-taking ability found in your own mind. Your mind can "take" the picture when nothing yet exists to be seen. Your dream can become a reality only if you first fix the picture of it in your mind. To visualize is to see it long before it is.

As I write this book, we are right in the midst of enor-mous success in the ministries of New Hope Community Church. We are experiencing exciting multiplication in both ministries and people. In the past year our atten-dance has jumped from below the first thousand to well above the second thousand. At this time our church enjoys over thirty need-meeting ministries to people. At age 31, I was a washout in the ministry. Now at age 43, I am enjoying the most challenging exciting time in the ministry that I could imagine.

The other day I was eating lunch with a friend and he said, "Dale, are you surprised at what's happening to New Hope?" My answer was, "Yes and no. Yes, I am amazed at God's goodness and all the miracles that he is working. But no, I'm not surprised at the large number of people coming and the multiplication of ministries because I visualized all of this happening ten years ago when New Hope was nothing but a God-given idea in my mind."

In the formative years of our New Hope dream, I gathered together our board and we formulated a vision of the property we would need in order to fulfill our God-given dream. Here is what we visualized and determined to have:

1. A spot of natural beauty on a lush green hillside.
2. Accessibility—close to the exits of a major freeway system and within fifteen minutes of 100,000 people.
3. Visibility—A piece of land that would have high exposure to thousands of people who would pass it every day on the freeway.
4. Ten acres or more—where we would have parking for thousands.
5. Developability—where sewers and water were in.

When we visualized this property, we had no idea where it was. But we saw it and in our vision we claimed it. We were to look at and explore dozens of properties before finding God's property for our dream.

Do you know where New Hope Community Church is located today? As I am writing this, I can look out the window of my corner office in our new building. The sanctuary seats 1200 worshipers, and the building has the needed supporting offices, educational facilities, and social and recreational facilities. This miracle building is located on ten-plus acres on a lush green hillside. As I sit here looking out my windows to the west, I see the I-205 Freeway. Directly across the freeway from us, I see the new Clackamas Town Center, its 175 stores making it the largest shopping center in the state of Oregon. Thousands upon thousands of people who enter the shopping center and who go up and down the freeway see the inspiring Cross of Hope lifted high into the air and the New Hope Church that has become a reality.

We are located one block off the Sunnyside exit. Our accessibility is such that within a range of ten minutes there are more than 100,000 people. On our east side, across the street from us, is a plush, green golf course. Our property is highlighted by surrounding green hillsides in the distance. We are blessed by towering trees around us. No church in the Northwest has a more choice location than we do.

God had a beautiful idea. We received and conceived and visualized that idea as a reality long before it was. And now it is a beautiful dream come true.

II. BELIEVE IT

Before you can see a dream come true, you must first see it and then you must believe it. In Mark 9:23 we are given these inspiring words: *If thou canst believe, all things are possible to him that believeth* (KJV).

No worthwhile dream is ever fulfilled until someone believes it can be done. The one thing that I had going for me when I started the ministry of New Hope was that I really believed in what I was doing with all my heart. So much so that I was willing to make a lifetime commitment to fulfilling this beautiful dream.

Someone has said, "If you believe you can do something, you will never give up because of obstacles. If you believe you cannot do something, you will be more inclined to give up early."

How true! Without belief not only do you give up early, but often you don't even get off the starting block.

Believing is knowing that it can be done somehow, somewhere, and at some time.
Believing is the magic word that can transform the impossible into the possible.

III. ACHIEVE IT

How do you see a dream come true? As we have already seen, first you conceive it, then you believe it, and then you move ahead to achieve it by getting started. The most difficult part of any project for me has been to take that first step and get started.

How do you get started? You stop putting off until tomorrow what you can do *now.* As long as you keep saying that tomorrow you are going to do it, tomorrow never comes. Procrastination is your enemy. Say these three words over and over until you are moved into immediate action: *Do it now!*

No dreams come true unless the dreamer is willing to work hard to make the dream a reality. Before you can reap the harvest, you must first sow the seeds. No worthwhile dream is ever accomplished easily. It takes some blood, sweat, and tears—not just for a day or a week or a month or a year, but often for years.

You must *deny the lesser to gain the greater.*

How do you make a beautiful dream come true? You keep on doing whatever it is you need to do, no matter which way the wind blows or how difficult the storm becomes. If your dream is worthwhile, then never, *never* give up.

Persistence is one of the finest qualities that any human being can have. When the going gets tough, the tough must get up and get going. Fight it through in the name of Jesus! *Those that see their dreams come true are ordinary people like you and me who exhibit an extraordinary amount of courage and determination.*

When you are trying to fulfill a beautiful dream, you can expect some setbacks and some time of discouragement. In those low moments you will be tempted to give up. During the Civil War, Abraham Lincoln once said, "If there is a worse place than hell, I'm in it."

Lincoln elected to stay with it until he had saved the Union. His dream cost him his life, but he saved our nation. In gratitude, every American loves the name of Abraham Lincoln.

What did Abraham Lincoln have? He had perseverance. So many times people come so close to fulfilling their dreams, but are defeated because they give up too soon. Let this verse of Scripture put staying power in your veins: *"Be ye steadfast, unmoveable, always abounding in the work of the Lord"* (1 Cor. 15:58, KJV).

If your dream is beautiful, if it's a God-given dream, if it will help other people, and if it brings the best out of you, then never, *never* give up. As long as you have the breath of life, *never give up!*

Because it's true. *Whatever the mind can conceive, and I will dare to believe, with God's help I can achieve.*

FOUR

DARE TO RISK FAILURE TO GAIN SUCCESS

I would rather attempt something great for God and fail than do nothing and succeed. Dr. Robert Schuller

You can enjoy many wonderful successes in your life if you're willing to risk failure, I'll be the first to admit that risking failure scares me. At the same time, what enormous joy comes in the adventure of trying to achieve something great! People who are reaching beyond to gain new heights are happy people.

As the eminent Swiss psychologist Paul Tournier says, "The joy of success is everything." Who are the men and women who enjoy success? They are the ones who are unafraid to challenge uncertainties and seek new horizons.

God told Abraham at the ripe old age of seventy-five to leave his home and go away into a strange land where God promised to bless and multiply him. Now, suppose Abraham had said, "I'm too old to do anything new." If he had entertained that kind of impossibility thinking, he would have stayed at home and missed the joy that he received from the adventure as well as the blessing of success. Abraham stands out in Bible history as a pioneer who risked failure to gain success. The Scripture describes it this way. *"Abraham obeyed. Away he went, not even knowing where he was going"* (Heb. 11:8, TLB). Can you imagine how difficult it must have been for a man seventy-five years of age to leave the security of his home and move away into an unknown land? What Abraham chose to do was not easy. No new adventure is ever an easy road to travel.

Why did Abraham take the risk? Because Abraham had a vision of doing greater things yet in his lifetime. The Bible says, *"Abraham did this because he was confidently waiting for God to bring him to that strong heavenly city whose designer and builder is God"* (Heb. 11:10, TLB). Abraham lived to the age of 175.

God has greater things yet for you to do.

AMBITION IS GOD'S GIFT TO YOU

Some wise person has said, "Ambition is that spur that makes men struggle with destiny; it is heaven's own incentive to make purpose great and achievement greater." It is ambition that makes us want to climb still higher.

Only in recent years have I come to understand clearly that ambition is a gift God has given to each of us. Ambition is not given to put us against each other. Neither is it given to make us step on top of one another as we try to make our way to the top. These are but the abuses and misuses of the gift of ambition that God has given.

Why has God given us this motivating gift? So that we might achieve good and wonderful things on this earth. I believe that just as each of us is uniquely different from the other; so each has a distinct work to accomplish on this earth. My friend, within you is planted the urge to fulfill your destiny. Whatever you do, don't waste your life away.

What is life like without ambition? One of the tragedies of our times is that so many young people have put their ambitions to death by using drugs. Without ambition for something more, people go nowhere fast. Ambition is that inner urge to reach toward the stars, to move onward and upward. It is this reaching beyond that puts zest and excitement into life. Yes, God, our heavenly Father, has given to each of us, his children, the gift of ambition to motivate us to accomplish beautiful things while we're here on earth.

To you God has given the gift of ambition to use for the good of mankind, and to fulfill your destiny to the glory of God.

NO GUARANTEED SUCCESS

Doesn't every person want to be a success? I know that there are a lot of people who play act today and try to put on the appearance that it doesn't matter to them whether they succeed or fail. Nevertheless, it does make a big difference. It makes the difference between feeling good about yourself and not feeling good about yourself. It makes the difference between getting the best things in life and settling for so much less. I confess it. I want to succeed. I want to be a successful father. I want to be a successful husband. I want to be a successful pastor. I want to be a successful friend. I want to accomplish some lasting good on this earth with the time that I have allotted to me.

When I was in the valley of decision making as to whether or not to risk failure in order to try to gain success in starting New Hope Community Church, I asked for and received a private meeting with my friend of many years, Dr. Robert Schuller. Without a doubt Dr. Schuller is the world leader in possibility thinking. His personality, messages, and writings have been a great inspiration to me.

Excited, and full of anticipation, I met with this great
man. In the maze of things that were happening and
weren't happening, I was trying to find God's will and
direction concerning my new dream. I thought if only
I could talk to Dr. Schuller he would give me all the
answers.

Dr. Schuller listened compassionately as I shared my
New Hope dream. But when I left him, I didn't have
any more answers than before we had the conversation.
By that night I was feeling very low emotionally. The
truth is, I was depressed. I had expected so much
and I felt as if I had gotten so little.

Weeks later I realized my big mistake. What I wanted
in Dr. Schuller was someone who would guarantee
that if I took the risk of launching New Hope Community
Church, I would be successful. That was something
no one could guarantee me.

A few days later I picked up once again one of
Dr. Schuller's books and I came across this famous line
which has come to mean so much to me. Here it is:

*I would rather attempt to do something great for God and
fail than do nothing and succeed.*

THERE IS NO SUCCESS WITHOUT RISKING FAILURE
Over the past months there has been an epidemic of
house break-ins in our neighborhood. These unnerving
robberies caused us to take some extra security pre-
cautions. The night after we had installed deadbolt locks
on all our doors, I was awakened in the middle of
the night by noises in our house. It sounded as if
someone had opened our front door and was walking
inside our entry way.

What would you do if a thief entered your house in
the middle of the night? I have never owned a gun,
so I couldn't defend myself that way. What could I do?

How could I protect my darling wife and my two little children?

I jumped up, and ran down the hallway as fast as I could to where the noise seemed to be coming from. Do you know what I did? I yelled as loud as I could—like a gorilla. I'd fix them! I'd scare them right out of the house.

Fortunately for me, the thief turned out to be our cat, Fluffy, playing with some trinkets and toys in our entry way.

There is something more fearful to me than having our home invaded. I confess that there is something that scares the wits out of me. This paralyzing fear almost stopped me dead from starting New Hope Community Church.

What is this fear that scares me to death? It is the fear of failure. Let's admit it, we all fear failure. Many a person has stopped before he or she ever started because of giving in to the fear of failure.

If there were no fear of failure, neither would there be any joy of success. Paul Tournier

To achieve the best things in your life, you must dare to risk a failure. There is no other way to succeed, and the alternative to making the choice to move ahead toward success is the unacceptable alternative of failing by doing nothing.

At our first New Hope Community Church office, "the upper room," an unforgettable poster hung in my small section. On this huge poster was a picture of a large green turtle and underneath were these appropriate words: *"BEHOLD THE TURTLE! HE MAKES PROGRESS ONLY WHEN HE STICKS HIS NECK OUT."*

God has written many lessons into the very core and design of nature to aid us in living successfully. I am convinced that, if for no other reason, God created the

turtle to teach you and me this unforgettable lesson:
Look at the turtle! Until he comes out of his shell and
sticks his neck out, he goes absolutely nowhere. All
forward progress for the turtle is dependent upon
sticking his neck out. What an important lesson! Until we
stick our necks out, we do not advance but instead
stand still.

When Margi and I started New Hope Community
Church, with Christ's help we stood up to our fears of
failure and in faith took the risk. There have been
so many successes during these ten years of high
adventure. And we anticipate that the best is yet to come!
But every time we have gained a new success, it has come
only after we dared to risk the failure. Whenever we
come to the point where we are no longer willing to take
the risk, at that moment we will stop moving toward
new success.

HOW DO YOU OVERCOME THE FEAR OF FAILURE?
You and I know how fear can scare the wits out of us.
What can we do to overcome fear?

The first thing to do is replace fear with faith. Refuse
to surrender to the fear of failure. When you start to
feel afraid, cancel it out with a faith statement or faith
thought. This requires applying Scripture to your life.
Condition your mind with faith-building Bible verses like
these:

The Lord is my Shepherd, I shall not want (Psa. 23:1, KJV).

*For God hath not given us the spirit of fear; but of power,
and of love, and of a sound mind* (2 Tim. 1:7, KJV).

*Be strong and of a good courage; be not afraid, neither be
thou dismayed: for the Lord thy God is with thee whither-
soever thou goest* (Josh. 1:9, KJV).

*When you go through deep waters and great trouble, I will
be with you. When you go through rivers of difficulty,
you will not drown! . . . For I am the Lord your God, your
Savior* (Isa. 43:2, 3, TLB).

The second thing to do is to stand up to your fears.
Emerson told us how any person could kill any fear
when he said, "Do the thing you fear, and the death of
fear is certain."

During my early boyhood years, our family used to take
vacations on a rainy lake in Minnesota. When I was
ten years old, one day my dad and the other men in camp
took high-powered speedboats and went twenty miles
up the lake seeking the big catch. They left me at home
to take my mother and three other ladies out fishing.
The little boat that I took the ladies in was old and
poorly equipped. But we didn't give it much thought
since we were just going a short distance from shore.

The sun was shining and everything seemed to be
going well. My guests were catching a few fish and I was
in my glory being the captain of the boat. Then suddenly
dark clouds started coming and the wind began to
blow and the waves churned. We found ourselves two
miles from shore and caught in a severe storm. My fun
turned to fear. The women aboard tried to act as if
they weren't scared, but the way they were clinging to the
sides of the little boat told a different story. Picture
the scene—a weak little boat caught in a mighty storm
with a ten-year-old inexperienced lad as captain.

Surrounded and overwhelmed by the storm and scared
out of my wits, I began to pray, asking Jesus to come to
my rescue. In that moment he gave me the courage
to stand up to my fears and head the little boat directly
into the big waves. With Christ's help I hit the waves
head on, took them one at a time, and made it safely to
shore. That day I learned a lesson I have never forgotten.

With Christ's help we can stand up to what we fear and overcome it with faith in action.

The third thing to remember is—Jesus' power is greater than any storm you will ever face. When the disciples were caught in the storm on the Sea of Galilee and were so afraid, Jesus came with his commanding, confident presence and said, *"It is I! Don't be afraid"* (Mark 6:50, TLB). And the wild, threatening sea became calm.

There are no storms he cannot calm.
There are no fears that Jesus cannot drive away.

Jesus is alive and has promised us, *"Lo, I am with you always even unto the end of the world"* (Matt. 28:20, KJV). Because his promise is true, not only can you stand up to the fear of failure, you can overcome it with faith.

Risking failure to gain success does not mean doing foolish things.

The young Christian banker called me on the phone and asked if we could have lunch together. Arrangements were made and we met at the appointed date. My impression was that here was an up-and-coming young man with a tremendous future in the field of banking. So I was somewhat unprepared when he announced to me that he had turned in his resignation to the bank president.

When I asked my friend why he had resigned his job, he explained to me that he had recently heard a sermon on faith at a convention and had decided to trust God completely. Without any more preparation than that, he was quitting his job to work just for the Lord and he knew somehow God would supply his needs.

I asked my pumped-up young friend a few worthy questions. "What are you planning to do for the Lord?"

Well, he wasn't too sure what he was going to do.
Next I asked, "How do you plan to support your family
and make the debt payments for which you are already
obligated?" Well, he hadn't given that too much thought,
but he guessed God would take care of him. I told my
young friend that I admired his enthusiasm in wanting to
do something for the Lord, but it was important to
follow sound biblical principles.

I then asked my friend if he liked his job. He replied,
"I like it better than anything I have ever done before."
I couldn't quite figure out what was going on until I asked
him about his family life. Then the hurt came pouring
out because things were very strained between him and
his wife. Being upset at home, he was trying to find an
escape.

"At this time more than any other, you need the
stability of your job to give your wife the feeling of security
she needs," I said. I suggested that Satan was using
his torn-up emotions to try and get him to do something
foolish, all in the name of faith. Not heeding my advice he
went ahead and quit his job. When I ran into him six
months later, he was separated, unemployed, frustrated,
and in his confusion, blaming God.

Faith is not foolishness. Faith is based on solid ground.
During an earlier pastorate, we once rented a private
picnic area with a large swimming pool. We'd hardly
gotten there when one of our five-year-old boys who
didn't know how to swim walked right out onto the
diving board and jumped off into the deep water. If it had
not been for a very alert lifeguard who rescued the
bold lad, he would have drowned. Before anyone is ready
to jump off the diving board, he has to first spend
hours in preparation learning how to swim.

One of the common characteristics of human nature is
that we are always wanting something for nothing.
I guess there is something of a gambler in all of us. The
risking of failure in order to gain success is not the

same thing as gambling. Rather, it is based on the solid ground of previous achievements, careful preparation, and being ready to take the next step upward in achievement. In other words, before you can do something big, you must succeed in smaller accomplishments.

You don't suddenly jump from the first level in the house up to the second level. How do you get to the upper level? You take the stairs one step at a time. Each step is a new risk, but that venture is built on the step you've taken and achieved before.

DON'T MISS THE BOAT

Don't forget: *"Of all the words of tongue or pen, the saddest are: it might have been"* (John Greenleaf Whittier). It has been said that if someone pulled back the curtain and we saw clearly the opportunities we have missed already in our lifetime, that would be hell.

A once-in-a-lifetime opportunity may be knocking at your door. The time to wake up is now. God wants to use you to do something grand.

If you are tired of not achieving very much in your life, then listen. The time has come for you to hear the words Jesus spoke to his disciples when they were empty-handed. Jesus said, *"Launch out into the deep—and let down your nets for a big catch"* (Luke 5:4).

I love these words, and I urge you to make them yours:

Grieve not for me, about to start a new adventure.
Eager I stand, ready to depart,
Me and my reckless pioneer heart.
—Author Unknown

FIVE

WHY BE OVERRUN WHEN YOU CAN OVERCOME?

God has no problems—only plans. Corrie ten Boom

Overcome or overcomer
Which one would you like to be?

In Morris West's novel, *The Shoes of the Fisherman*, the dominant character is the pope. One night, not long after his coronation, the pope goes out for a walk and wanders into one of the poorest sections of Rome. He is dressed in a simple cassock, and so passes unrecognized by the people he meets. As he walks along, a door in an apartment house opens and a man rushes out, running smack into the pope and almost knocking him down. The man mutters an apology and then, as he catches sight of the cassock, says curtly, "There's a man dying up there. Maybe you can do more for him than I can."

"Who are you?" asks the interested pope.

"A doctor," replied the man. "They never call us until it's too late." The pope goes into the house and finds a man who obviously is at the point of death. He is alone except for a young woman who is nursing him. The pope tries to talk to the dying man, but there is no response. The girl says, "It's no use, Father. He's too far gone to hear you." The pope pronounces the absolution and kneels to pray. Soon the man is dead.

The woman says, "We should go, Father, neither of us will be welcome now."

"I would like to help the family," says the pope.

"We should go," the woman says again. Then she adds in one of the unforgettable lines of the book, "They can cope with death; it's only living that defeats them."

I find this line from Morris West's novel to be haunting. Today people are overwhelmed and overrun by what appear to be unsolvable problems. Vast numbers of people are victims of what I call "the problem complex." They have become convinced that their difficulties or circumstances are unsolvable and insurmountable, so they are destined to live a defeated life.

In the summer of 1980 we were right in the middle of our huge building project when interest rates hit an all-time high of 20 percent. This caused us multiple problems. There was the problem of not being able to borrow enough money for the project. There was the problem of having to pay extremely high interest rates for the money we were able to borrow. And the $200,000 cash we had counted on from the land sale of our Sunnyside Road property was past due and looked impossible to collect. I confess to you that I felt some panic. We were being overrun and overcome by circumstances beyond our control.

During this heavy time I received a letter from one of our dear members, Eileen Burke, who was away visiting in California. Eileen used this letter to minister to me in such a beautiful way. Here's some of what Eileen wrote:

Your letter marked urgent *was sent to me in California at my daughter's. I am sorry for the financial distress.*

But at the same time am confident that God will make a
way where there seems to be no way. I am reminded of
a quote from Corrie ten Boom—"God has no problems—
only plans."

What had been happening to me was that I was getting
all bogged down in the quicksand of the problems.
I was fast losing sight of the plans. Whatever is happening
to your life, remember, God has no problems—only
plans. Whatever you do, don't lose sight of the plan.

God has a plan for your life. And the plan is that no
matter what comes, no matter how difficult your
circumstances become, no matter what tragedies strike,
you are not to become a helpless victim. Through
God's power and strength you are to rise up and be the
victor. I believe that in the power of Christ we can
overcome anything and everything that would defeat us.

Jesus said, *"If ye have faith as a grain of mustard*
seed, ye shall say unto this mountain, Remove hence to
yonder place; and it shall remove; and nothing shall
be impossible unto you" (Matt. 17:20, KJV).

With Christ we don't have to mope.
We don't have to give up hope.
We can face obstacles and cope.

Yes, and then, *"We are more than conquerors through*
him that loved us" (Rom. 8:37, KJV).

SEVEN THINGS TO DO TO OVERCOME ANY
PROBLEM AND EVERY OBSTACLE THAT COMES
IN YOUR LIFE
STEP 1: OPEN YOUR EYES TO SEE BEYOND
One of our common shortcomings as human beings is
that we are always losing our perspective. Our teenager
gets kicked out of school, and suddenly we think

the whole world has caved in on us. All we can see and feel is that our child is in big trouble. What we need to do is lift up our sights and see beyond—see that the final chapter has not been written. Yes, there is a crisis that needs to be dealt with. But with God's help we can see the bigger picture. We can see the goal is to help the child grow up and become a responsible Christian citizen. Along the way of life you may lose many battles, but you can still win the war.

When overwhelming problems come into your life, what do you do? When the problems are compounded and you are under the pile, what do you do? First of all, don't panic! You say, "That's easy for you to say, but how do you do it?" Lift up your eyes to God who is bigger than anything that has gone wrong in your life. When the storms are raging, be still and know that he is God.

God is still in control.

Trust in the God of the impossible. I understand that to you your situation seems impossible, but let me remind you that with God all things are possible.

And God can move a mighty mountain.

STEP 2: STAND UP AND FACE YOUR PROBLEMS
They called him "the iron horse." Year after year, injured or well, Lou Gehrig never missed a game for the New York Yankees. He played with lumbago, a concussion, even broken bones.

Then, at the start of the 1939 season, Lou suddenly became slow and awkward in the field, ineffectual at bat. In a game with the Washington Senators, he went to bat four times and never even knicked the ball. He also muffed an easy throw. That's when he told manager, Joe McCarthy, "I guess the time has come to take me out." His consecutive game record ended at 2,130, a record that may never be equaled.

Doctors discovered that Lou had a rare and fatal disease called *amyotrophic lateral sclerosis*. The next two years, as life ebbed from him, he refused to give in to the disease.

On July 4, 1939, they honored Lou at Yankee Stadium. The spectators fell silent as Gehrig stepped to the microphone, and said, "I may have been given a bad break, but I've got an awful lot to live for. I consider myself the luckiest man on the face of the earth." It was the most heartwarming and inspiring moment in the history of baseball.

Courage is one of the finest, most dynamic of human values. Unfortunately it appears to be lacking in a lot of people's lives today. Without courage people give up when faced with a difficult problem. Instead of standing up to what they fear, they run and hide.

When the going gets tough, have you ever felt like giving up? I have. More than once when the load got heavy I felt like running away. Sooner or later difficult circumstances come to everyone. And when they come to you, you face a big choice. You can either be overrun or you can, through Christ Jesus, find courage and stand up and overcome.

This verse is for you. *"Be strong! Be courageous! . . . For the Lord your God will be with you. He will neither fail you nor forsake you"* (Deut. 31:6, TLB).

STEP 3: BELIEVE THERE IS A SOLUTION TO EVERY PROBLEM

Just as there is for every night a day, there is for every problem a solution. Problems have a purpose. Every advance our civilization has ever made came as a direct result of solving a problem. When you're faced with a problem, it's not time to throw up your hands in despair. It's time to dig in and use your energies and the creative mind that God has given you to solve the problem. You were created to be a problem solver. In every problem that comes into your life, you face the choice of either becoming a part of the problem or part of the solution.

I know that you want to be a problem solver. To be a problem solver, you must train your mind so that whenever you are faced with a problem, your mind begins to immediately look for a solution. Did you know that most problems have not only one solution but many different solutions?

In every problem there is a possibility.

Once when Jesus went out into the wilderness, 5,000 men followed him. Besides these 5,000 men there were probably an additional 15,000 women and children —a grand total of 20,000 followers. As evening approached, the multitudes of people were hungry after listening to Jesus teach all day. The people had gone after Jesus without having made provisions for food to eat. Thus, a giant problem—20,000 starving people and no food to feed them.

Christ called Philip, one of his disciples, and asked him by what means they were going to feed the multitude. Philip, whom I characterize as an impossibility thinker, responded by pointing out all the reasons it was impossible. Do you know that anyone can be an impossibility thinker? Philip was full of reasons why it couldn't be done. "We aren't in downtown Jerusalem; there isn't any place to buy food; if there were, we don't have enough money to buy all the food it would take to feed the multitude."

While Philip was verbalizing to Jesus all the reasons it couldn't be done, Andrew overheard. Being a possibility thinker, Andrew began to open his mind to explore all the possibilities. When faced with a big problem, the best thing you can do is open your eyes to explore all the possibilities for solving the problem.

Just between you and me, I love Andrew. Andrew saw in some of the smallest things the biggest possibilities. He found a little boy with five loaves of bread and two fishes. The natural response is, "Andrew, that's not anything. That's not going to solve such a big problem. You might say that's like trying to satisfy the appetite of an elephant by feeding him one ant. Andrew, it's nice you want to help, but you're just whistling Dixie."

But Andrew, the possibility thinker, refused to allow anything to dampen or wipe out his faith. He believed that with God anything was possible. So he brought what he had to Jesus—the boy with five loaves and two fishes.

Jesus asked the boy for what he had. The boy gave it. Jesus took the seed of bread and fishes and he worked the miracle of the harvest. And all 20,000 people were not only fed but were filled up, and there were baskets left overflowing in abundance.

There is no problem too big for God whenever he can get his disciples to be possibility thinkers.

STEP 4: EXPECT OBSTACLES
Any time you set out to accomplish something that is worthwhile, you are going to encounter obstacles. And the more worthwhile your goal, the more obstacles you can expect. Did you hear that? Do you want to do something great for God? That is wonderful. But the greater your project is, the bigger the giants you're going to have to face. The fact that you are doing God's will does not mean it will be easy. The Bible teaches us that one cannot even be a follower of Jesus without encountering some opposition and obstacles. As the Apostle Paul experienced, you can expect some

tribulation, some distress, and at times, persecution. But, *"We are more than conquerors through him that loved us"* (Rom. 8:37, KJV).

Jesus faced insurmountable obstacles—a veritable mountain range of problems. His own family did not understand his life and mission and tried to stop him in his ministry. The religious leaders in his day, instead of giving him a place to preach, became his enemies and set out both secretly and openly to destroy him. Yet without buildings, without even a public address system, Jesus got his transforming message of love into the hearts of scores of people. Even when facing death itself, he faced it head on, dying on a cross to be resurrected and to become victor over the obstacle of death itself.

Jesus, the victor, is our leader in overcoming anything and everything.

If you are going to do something great for God, you can expect opposition. Not everyone is going to approve and understand what it is you are trying to accomplish.

At every point of development of New Hope Community Church, there were people who disagreed with what I was trying to lead the church in accomplishing. You can expect it. Be kind to your opposition. But do not allow them to make you forget who you are and what God has called you to accomplish. Learn everything you can from your critics, but do not let them destroy your God-given dream.

STEP 5: IN EVERY ADVERSITY
LOOK FOR THE STRIKING OPPORTUNITY
When the obstacle arises, when the adversity strikes, you are faced with a choice. You can throw up your hands, lie down, and let it defeat you, or you can look for the striking opportunity.

In the history and development of New Hope Community Church, we have faced and overcome giant obstacles. In the first eight years of ministry, not having a building of our own, we worshiped in eleven different places: drive-in theaters, inside theaters, nursery schools, school buildings, other people's churches.

In my experience it has not been easy to rent a facility in which to hold a church. You don't simply walk into a place and walk out again with the keys in your pocket. It often takes weeks, even months, to get the prospective renter willing to open the doors to your ministry.

Thirteen months after launching the need-meeting ministry of New Hope in the Eighty-Second Avenue Drive-In Theater, we were shut out. On Friday afternoon, December 14, 1973, I received an unwanted greeting:

This letter is to notify you that we do not wish to continue our premises for your use for church service as of January 1, 1974. It has been nice knowing you.

From 1975 to 1977 we had the good fortune of being able to rent a neighborhood denominational church building on King Road. For the first time we had our offices, activities, and worship all under one roof. Soon after we began using the facility, the denominational church went out of business and left us as sole occupants. There we began to develop some of the ministries that we had not been able to carry on before, such as youth work, children's ministries, and a lay pastors' program. There we began to grow up as a church. The ministry was going well. Then we received notice that the building had been sold. Within thirty days we were to be out. Once again God was teaching us that the church was something more than a building.

I talked the principal of the Wichita Grade School on King Road into letting us hold church services in

the school. He was a very congenial administrator, and we
got very excited about our potential for growth in
the school. There we would have the classrooms and
auditorium space to grow and expand significantly.
We didn't have a lot of people at that time, but we had a
big vision.

The first Sunday we looked pretty small in that big
gymnasium. But each Sunday the attendance was
increasing. Our future was looking bright. We had been in
the Wichita School for two months when I came home
one Friday to an upset wife. Quickly Margi told me that
she had just received a call from the superintendent
of schools in the district and he wanted to see me
immediately.

I walked into his office. It didn't take him long after the
formal greeting to drop the bomb. He said, "We want
you out of the school now." Then he explained that he
had been unaware of our being in the Wichita School
and that it was the school board's policy not to let
churches into schools. My begging and pleading for just
one more Sunday were to no avail. We were kicked out
—now!

I heard just the other day that after all these years
the school board has reversed itself and is now renting
the schools to churches. Praise the Lord for that
change in policy.

After being put out of the school, we were forced to
move quite a distance into the central part of southeast
Portland to rent an Adventist church. It was a lovely,
well-kept, older building that accommodated about 200
people. The Adventists were very nice people to work
with. Here the ministry really began to thrive, and
our attendance doubled the first year we were in the
Adventist church. We were starting to really push the
walls out with our attendance when on a Saturday
morning in November 1977, fire broke out and gutted the
church. The bad news was that we were once again
without a church home. The good news for us was that

had it burned on Sunday we would have been responsible to pay for the loss.

Because of the tremendous growth that we were experiencing in the Adventist church, I had already begun negotiating with the president of Warner Pacific College at Southeast Sixty-Eighth and Division in Portland for the rental of their commodious and modern chapel. Prior to the fire our negotiations had been deadlocked. But on the day of the fire I called him up, told him of our predicament, and asked if we could move in the next day. Being a man of God, he saw our need, responded with open arms, and let us move in.

Moving into Warner Pacific College was a big step of faith. At that time we were running approximately 200 people on Sunday mornings and moving into a facility that would seat 800. Previously we had been paying $100 a Sunday to rent. Now we committed ourselves to paying $400 a Sunday in rent. During the two-and-a-half years we were privileged to use the Warner Pacific chapel, our attendance and membership increased two-and-a-half times. God helped us to build the kind of base and enlarge the ministry to the point that we could fulfill our dream of building our first church large enough to minister to thousands of unchurched people.

Right in the midst of our decision making process as to whether to move ahead and build our own building or wait, I received a cordial letter from the new president of Warner Pacific College. He explained that there were changing conditions at the college and invited us to please leave by January 1, 1981. This date he had set allowed just the amount of time it would take to begin and complete the building of our own church home.

Shut out, sold out, kicked out, burned out, and invited out! At the time each of these happened it seemed like an overwhelming obstacle. It appeared that we had no place to go, and the larger the ministry became, the more difficult it became to find a suitable place. And yet, every time we were forced to move, God helped us to find a bigger and better place. And every time we moved, the people moved with us. And the wonderful thing was that every time we moved, not only did the people move with us, but more people came and found New Hope a reality in their lives.

How did this happen? Because every time we suffered a setback, we began immediately to look for the striking opportunity.

When you suffer a setback, don't sit around feeling sorry for yourself, but get up and look for something greater to do.

The best defense is a good offense.

Through all of these obstacles God taught us, led us, used us, and prepared us for the great things that were to come.

Nothing is impossible with God!

STEP 6: SEE TRYING TIMES AS TIMES TO TRIUMPH
Did you know that Christianity is strong stuff? There is nothing sissy about it. The truth is, it can make strong men out of sissies. It can turn frightened women into strong women of courage. Christianity can put the brace in your back when you need to stand firm in the midst of the storm. Faith in Jesus can keep you going when physically and emotionally you feel like giving up.

Never settle for defeat.

I'll never forget the first anniversary of our New Hope Community Church. The only morning service that we had was held in the drive-in theater. One thing about doing a service in a drive-in theater: we were subject to all the same kinds of setbacks that people experience in their lives. The night before our first anniversary, one of the drunks leaving the drive-in movie knocked over several sound posts which disabled the sound system.

Ironically the sermon topic I had chosen for the day was, "Trying Times Are Times to Triumph." That Sunday morning when Margi and I got up, even though the forecast was for rain, we did not allow that to dampen our spirits. With joyful anticipation we drove to the theater, looking forward to celebrating our first anniversary of the ministry. Upon arrival we were told that we had no sound. And just at the appointed time to start the service, the rains came pouring down.

What do you do when everything goes wrong? I can tell you what I felt like doing—getting into my car and going back home and forgetting I had ever heard of a drive-in church. But that morning I had an opportunity to live what I was preaching. So I had the ushers get the cars in as close to me as possible and asked the people to roll their windows down a little bit. Then I stood and shouted at the top of my voice God's message for the moment, "Trying Times Are Times to Triumph." I'm sure that those of us who were there that day will never forget the victory that came out of what looked like sure defeat.

Hard times can be the best times. Trying times are times to stand up and triumph. Throw yourself whole-heartedly into the challenge. As someone has suggested triumph is TRY-UMPH.

When the going gets tough, the tough get going.

STEP 7: ACCEPT GOD'S POWER
AND OVERCOME ANYTHING AND EVERYTHING
During these past nine years of New Hope ministry, I admit to times of doubt and discouragement. These times have come when my emotional, physical, and spiritual strength has been depleted. In that lonely moment away from the crowd, the thing which I have

visualized and announced to the people with great faith has not seemed so sure. I have been hit by the discouraging darts of doubt.

In such times these words are brought to me again by the Spirit of the Lord.

But they that wait upon the Lord shall renew their strength. They shall mount up with wings like eagles; they shall run and not be weary; they shall walk and not faint (Isa. 40:31, TLB).

Then after I had waited and allowed my spirit to be renewed by his Spirit, these words would come to rebuild my faith and courage: *"Not by might, nor by power, but by my spirit, saith the Lord of hosts"* (Zech. 4:6, KJV).

How are we going to do great things for God? Not by mere human calculation, not by just our own efforts, but with God's power we are going to overcome obstacles and be victorious.

The story is told that John Wesley, the founder of the Methodist Church, was once talking to a farmer friend out in the country. They saw a cow with its head over a stone wall, looking off into the distance. Wesley said to the farmer, "Suddenly I am perplexed by a question. Why would that cow be looking over the wall?"

The farmer answered, "Well, that's simple; she's looking over the wall because she can't see through it."

In your life you have obstacles, problems, setbacks, disappointments, seeming impossibilities. At the moment it may seem that God is not around. It seems that there is no way through. In such times, when you can't see your way through, look up, look to Jesus. How powerful, how strong he is! Fix your eyes on Jesus. And when you do, you will see over the wall and have the faith to stop being a victim and become a victor.

We are more than conquerors through him that loved us!

SIX
WALKING WOUNDED

I will seek that which was lost, and bring again that which was driven away, and will bind up that which was broken, and will strengthen that which was sick (Ezek. 34:16, KJV).

He said he loved you, promised he would be with you in sickness and health 'til death do you part. Now after twenty-three years of marriage, he has left you for another woman. You feel betrayed and cheated out of the best years of your life. You are hurting.

They have been your best friends for the past ten years. You've even taken vacations together. Now they are avoiding you. You don't understand what has happened, but you know that you are being rejected. And it hurts. Boy, does it hurt.

You gave your son the best of everything. You sacrificed to give him all the things you never had. You spent thousands of dollars putting him through college and medical school. You poured all your unfulfilled dreams into his life. Now he is a wealthy, successful doctor living in another state. Months go by and you don't hear a word from him. Last Christmas when you went to visit, he acted as if he was embarrassed to have you around. You hurt so deeply that you are not sleeping well at night.

Many things happen along the path of life to hurt us, but the worst hurt comes from the people we love the most.

"In war, there are no unwounded soldiers."[1] It is also true that in the arena of life not one of us escapes being hurt and wounded. A practicing psychologist friend of mine estimates that for every physical illness we suffer there are forty-five to sixty emotional hurts that wound us and cause us pain.

There are hurts from friends.
There are hurts from a marriage mate.
There are hurts from children.
There are hurts from employers and employees.
There are hurts from enemies.
There are hurts from failures.
There are hurts from losses.
There are self-inflicted hurts.

All of these hurts leave us wounded. Getting hurt is a part of being human. Have you ever hurt another human being? I have often made the statement that I would not intentionally hurt another human being for the world. Yet, I keep discovering that I *have* hurt other people. Oftentimes the people I have hurt are the ones that I love the very most. Admit it, you are not any holier than I am. Now, if you and I both hurt other people, why are we so surprised when we get hurt by another human being?

One of my dear friends is Merle Peterson, who is now ninety years of age. Merle is a booster of mine, and I always enjoy her keen mind. A few days ago I received a note from her in which she shared this insight, "It

is human nature to hurt others when we are angry
and hurt."

This reminded me of a story I heard about the tigers
in Asia. Ordinarily tigers will not attack people. However,
when a tiger is hurt, it will leave its natural habitat
and go after human beings, seeking to do them in.

In a small village in the heart of the jungle, one of the
villagers spotted a limping tiger on the prowl. Quickly
he sounded the alarm and all the villagers ran and
hid underneath their mud huts. Fearing for their lives
they lay side by side in silence. Suddenly the stillness was
broken by the hideous moaning and groaning of the
wounded tiger as he went prowling through the village.

Early the next morning the village men gathered
and quickly set off on a hunt to track down the wounded
tiger. When they had cornered the animal, they shot
him with their dart guns and put him out of his misery.
Upon examining the dead tiger, they found a deep
wound in his left paw. It was filled with pus and festering
from infection.

The tiger who was hurting and wounded was on the
prowl to hurt and wound others. This tiger is not the only
walking wounded. Our world has become filled with
people who are walking wounded. They have deep hurts
and the wounds are infected and going unhealed.

Unhealed hurts become deeply infected wounds.

Gary and Joy Lafe, our Minister of Music and his lovely
wife, are our friends and fellow workers. They are
doing a fantastic job of leading our church in the ministry
of music. They both not only know music, but have
beautiful spiritual gifts that enhance their ministry of
music to our congregation. When the Lafes came to
us three years ago, they were deeply wounded. A few
days ago when I interviewed Gary, he opened himself up
to share his wounds and the healing that has been

happening in him and his lovely wife. My thanks to Gary and Joy for making themselves vulnerable in sharing out of their own lives in order that God might help you with your hurts.

DALE: What was your inner condition when you came to be on staff at New Hope in October 1979?

GARY: I had a lot of hurts in my life at that time. We had, both Joy and I, gone through a very traumatic experience in a former staff position in California. We were really hurting, and we needed to receive healing. At the same time I knew the Lord wanted me to continue in the ministry.

DALE: How was this hurting affecting you personally, your marriage relationship, and your ability to serve the Lord?

GARY: I think it was detrimental in all three areas. It definitely was affecting our family situation and our home life. Our marriage at that time was probably at one of its lowest ebbs because of the stress we felt. It also affected my ability to minister to other people because I needed healing inside before I could share that love and that healing with somebody else. So I was a mess.

DALE: One thing I've observed is that when a married couple are both wounded, it's really difficult for them to help each other. Did you experience something like that?

GARY: That's right. I was hurting so badly that when Joy would reach out to me, I couldn't help her. And when I would reach out to Joy, she couldn't help me. There was nothing really left inside of us. We had given out and we were hurting too much to respond to each other.

DALE: When you're that wounded, too, it really gets tough to minister, doesn't it?

GARY: It really does. It's hard to reach out to somebody else because you're so centered on your own problems

and your own hurts. In fact I had gone to a church
where I was trying out and I had to preach at an evening
service. It was the worst thing I have ever done in
my life. I came away feeling very low about myself
because I knew I had done a miserable job. There was
nothing I could give.

DALE: How did you find healing; how did it happen?
Was it an instant thing or was your healing progressive?

GARY: It was a very progressive, long, slow process,
and we are still in that process. We had to come to a crisis
point in our relationship. Coming to New Hope forced
us to take a look at our own relationship and where
we were. It forced me to take a look at my ministry. Out
of that we made some specific choices of how we
were going to get healed. It involved some counseling, it
involved a lot of love and compassion from you,
Dale, and other staff people. We were surrounded by love
and that healing influence of love began to heal the
wounds. I think our wounds had to be exposed before
they could be healed.

DALE: That's true, isn't it? You have to expose the
wounds before they can be healed. As long as you are
hiding them, no healing takes place, does it?

GARY: That's right. We were definitely trying to cover
up what was going on. No way did we want people
to know what was happening, because I believed if that
happened I would lose my position. I would lose
everything that the Lord had called me to do. So there
was a lot of fear along with everything else.

DALE: That's probably one of the big reasons people
do not expose their wounds. They are afraid that
other people wouldn't accept them if they knew. But
there is no way you can be healed unless you open up.
So the first step, I guess, in your healing was exposing
your wounds and beginning to open up. How did you
deal with feelings that you had inside? Did you have any
ill feelings? What happened next?

GARY: I had some bitterness from my experience

earlier and I had to deal with that. There was a time later
on in the year when I had to sit down with the person
that I had bitter feelings toward and talk that out and ask
forgiveness for those bitter feelings. It ended up in a
beautiful healing, and I think that was one of the main
beginnings for me personally in the healing process.
But I had to be honest about my own feelings, first of all,
and say, "I'm in trouble. I need help." That was the
hardest place for me to come to because it was a very
humbling experience.

I had to really want to be healed. You know, to the
point that I was willing to do whatever it took.

DALE: It's interesting that when Jesus healed people,
he made them do something that said, "Hey, I *want*
to be healed."

GARY: You and I had an encounter on the beach. That
was a difficult experience for me, opening up to
you and saying, "I need help. I'm hurting." I was never
willing to do that before. I wanted the healing, but
I wasn't willing to do what it took to get it, to say I
needed it.

DALE: Together we practiced the healing principles
given to us in James, *"Admit your faults to one another
and pray for each other so that you may be healed"*
(Jas. 5:16, TLB). And on that day God began his healing
within you.

GARY: He sure did!

DALE: How has the healing that you have experienced
over these months and years affected your relationship
with your wife and your ministry?

GARY: I think it has brought everything to the point
I have wanted it to be. I always dreamed about the
kind of relationship that I now have with my wife and my
family, with the church staff, and in my ministry. I
think it's just the beginning right now of better things to
come.

Joy and I are able to communicate as we've never been
able to communicate before. We are able to reach out to

each other. When she's hurting, I can be sensitive to
her. And she's sensitive to me. That has never happened
in our relationship before.

I see my ministry in all areas growing. People
responding. It's unique. Because of the experiences I've
gone through in my own married life and my struggles
in the last four or five years, I am sensitive to people who
are having similar experiences. I am better able to
help other people.

DALE: How has all of this affected your wife?

GARY: Well, she is full of joy! She's kind of getting
bubbly and giddy and she's feeling good about herself.
She's feeling good about me as her husband and as
the leader of the home. It's great to see that in her
because I haven't seen that since the time we were
courting.

DALE: It's so neat to see Joy come out of the shell and
be free in her own self and in her spirit, to have joy
that just flows. That's neat.

GARY: It sounds like a small thing, but one of the key
things in our relationship right now is that we are
happy. I'm happy in my home relationship. I'm happy in
my ministry. And if one doesn't have that, then he
is not much to anybody.

DALE: What happens is that when you are hurting, you
can't be happy. So when you are healed, then you
can be free in the Spirit and really begin to enjoy the
abundant life Jesus came to give you.

The church is to be a loving, healing fellowship.

All healing comes from God. One of the things that God
has been teaching me is that he uses different
instruments to deliver his healing. He uses doctors
and nurses; he uses psychologists and counselors;
and he uses ministers and compassionate Christian
workers.

While God uses a variety of sources to bring healing

into our lives, there is no other agency more equipped and chosen by God to heal people's hurts and make broken persons whole than the church of Jesus Christ.

In God's plan, his church is to be a healing fellowship, a place where sick people are getting well. Never have there been more people deeply hurt and wounded than right now. This is the day for the people of God to rise up and become God's instrument of healing to the walking wounded.

Unbelievable authority for ministering healing to one another in Jesus' name is given to us by our Lord in the Scripture, *"Whatsoever ye shall bind on earth shall be bound in heaven: and whatsoever ye shall loose on earth shall be loosed in heaven"* (Matt. 18:18, KJV).

In this exciting passage, Jesus promises that wherever two or three gather in his name, he will be there. And where Jesus is, there is power—power to heal hurts and to make broken lives whole again.

At New Hope Community Church we have put into practice this healing principle found in James 5:16, *"Admit your faults to one another and pray for each other so that you may be healed"* (TLB). From this Scripture we see three things that are to happen when Christians come together in the name of Jesus in the spirit of love, acceptance, and forgiveness. First, in the atmosphere of love we find we can open up and admit our faults to one another. Second, in the spirit of love and acceptance and forgiveness, we respond by praying immediately for the confessed need. Third, together in faith we claim the forgiveness, cleansing, and healing of God's love.

Last month at one of our home Bible fellowship groups that Margi and I were attending, there was a woman in her thirties who came for the first time in months to the fellowship. A few hours before coming she had received word that her brother had committed suicide. When she came into the house, she looked as sad as any person could look. In acceptance and love, our hearts went out to her.

We asked her to share with us what had happened. Her emotions were so strong that she could not even speak. Lovingly we gathered around and placed our hands on her. For the next thirty minutes in prayer and meditation we ministered love to her and in the name of Jesus healed her. When she left that night, she looked like a completely different person from the one who had walked in. When she said good night to everyone, she had confidence in her face and a warm smile. And in the days following she experienced a peace and comfort inside that held her despite having to face a very difficult family time at the funeral.

As leader of New Hope Community Church, what I desire most in the entire ministry of this church is a loving atmosphere. That is something we have, and I am committed with everything that is within me to maintaining it. It is a place where people can come and feel the presence of Jesus because they know they are being accepted, loved, and forgiven.

How do you teach this to Christians in any church? The answer is simple. The leadership must begin by confessing their own faults and weaknesses and asking people to pray for them that they might be healed.

Only when Christian leaders are healed can they be used to heal others.
Only when you have received the gift of love can you give others the gift of love.

WHAT CAN HEAL MY HURTS?
The other day a man asked me this direct question—what can heal my hurts? The man had a lot of hurts. He was convinced that he had been taken advantage of in an unfair business deal. He had been wronged by a

close friend. His own children had hurt him deeply.

To my friend I said, "I know what it is to be hurt. To be cut to the core. To be wounded so deeply that you are not sure you are going to make it. In 1970 I was deeply hurt by being rejected and divorced. I was hurt by the misunderstandings of friends that came as a result. I had a lot of hurt and pain that I would feel for years in not belonging to the church of my birth. I have had the hurt of not being accepted in a lot of evangelical circles because I have been divorced and remarried. I've had the pain of not seeing my two older children for months at a time and missing the experiences of their growing up. Yes, my friend, I know what it is to be one of the walking wounded.

"But, my friend, I'm glad to tell you that there is no hurt that has ever come to me but which to this day has been healed. I don't hurt anymore. The wounds have all been healed. And the same God who has brought healing in my life is ready to heal all your hurts."

"Out of your weakness shall come strength" [See Heb. 11:34].

There is something that you need to know. Your hurts will not automatically heal themselves. If you are going to live a healthy, happy emotional life, then you are going to have to learn how to handle your hurts and get them healed.

**EIGHT THINGS YOU CAN
DO TO HEAL ALL YOUR HURTS**
1. COME INTO THE PRESENCE OF JESUS
The Bible says of Jesus that he was *"a man of sorrows and acquainted with grief"* (Isa. 53:3, KJV). That means he knew what it was to hurt. He knew firsthand what it was

to be crushed. No one has ever been more mistreated, rejected, and abused than he was. According to all that modern psychiatry teaches, when you consider all the hurts he experienced, Jesus should have been a hopeless, maladjusted misfit.

Instead, Jesus Christ was the healthiest, strongest, most stable, total man who has ever lived. He was completely well and whole on the inside because there was a continual flow of healing throughout his being. Jesus, the whole one, is the healer of the world.

Jesus came to make broken people whole.

In the Scriptures we read, *"There is salvation in no other name than Jesus"* [See Acts 4:12]. The word, *salvation* comes from a Greek word meaning, *"to make whole."* Jesus came not only to forgive sins and heal the sick, but to heal the hurts of the brokenhearted.

Yes, Jesus came working the miracles of healing. He made the lame to walk, the blind to see, the dead to live, the oppressed to be freed, and the broken to be healed. Nothing is impossible with Jesus. And the Scriptures tell us, *"Jesus Christ is the same yesterday, today, and forever"* (Heb. 13:8, TLB). The same Jesus that walked this earth, working miracles back in Bible days is alive and working miracles now.

There is healing in Jesus' name.

Visualize Jesus. Use the God-given power inside your mind to picture Jesus. See him compassionate, strong, inviting you to come boldly into his presence.

2. EXPOSE YOUR WOUNDS TO JESUS
John Powell said, "When you repress or suppress those things which you don't want to live with, you don't really

solve the problem, because you don't bury the problem dead—you bury it alive. It remains alive and active in you!"

Before any hurt can be healed, you must open it up to Jesus. We get so in the habit of playing hide-and-seek with our hurts. We hide our hurts and secretly wish someone would come and find us and help us to stop hurting.

The time has come to stop playing this childish game. Jesus Christ himself stands with open arms waiting for you. Unconditionally he loves you and accepts you in your pain. His compassionate heart of love reaches out this moment to receive you.

Walk boldly into his presence and open up your hurt to him. Talk it out, cry it out, shout it out. Do whatever you need to do. But make sure you get it all out.

I heard about a preacher who was down on his knees behind his desk, praying to God and getting it all out. An eavesdropper overheard this confession, "Lord, your competition has made me a very tempting offer to go to work for him." Now that's what I call getting honest and really opening up to the Lord.

3. CONFESS YOUR HURT AND WHATEVER ELSE YOU NEED TO CONFESS

Healing begins with confession. Without the confession of hurt, there is no healing of the hurt.

True confession means you stop pointing the finger and playing the blame game. No matter how unjustly another person has wounded you, you must become responsible for your own attitude and spirit. For you to harbor ill feelings toward that person is a sin. If there is any trace of resentment, bitterness, or hatred in you, you will not heal until you accept responsibility for it and confess it as being wrong in your life.

Confession is good for what ails you.

4. EXTEND TO THE ONE WHO HAS HURT YOU THE SAME FORGIVENESS YOU HAVE RECEIVED FROM GOD

Jesus said, *"For if ye forgive men their trespasses, your heavenly Father will also forgive you; but if ye forgive not men their trespasses, neither will your Father forgive your trespasses"* (Matt. 6:14, 15, KJV).

Think with me for a moment. What if there were no forgiveness? Suppose when Jesus was being tortured on the cross, falsely accused, and unjustly crucified, he had refused to forgive us our sins. Where would we be if Jesus had not spoken those words, *"Father, forgive them, for they know not what they do"* (Luke 23:34, KJV)?

A couple of months ago I received a letter from a woman in a neighboring western state. She had just watched one of our New Hope TV telecasts over CBN.

In the letter she openly shared that at one time she'd been a pastor's wife. She had rebelled against God and her up bringing, had been involved with another man, and left her minister husband.

It had all begun so innocently, talking to another man who was understanding and sharing moments together. But emotional attachment led to expressing physical appreciation, and she found herself pregnant with a child of her new lover. Her sin destroyed her marriage, destroyed her husband's ministry, and damaged a lot of innocent people.

Before you cast the first stone, remember, *"All have sinned and come short of the glory of God"* (Rom. 3:23, KJV). Oh, my heart goes out to a hurting person like this one. Whether another person has hurt you or you have inflicted hurt on yourself, it still hurts. Maybe it hurts even more when you know you've done it to yourself.

I'm glad to tell you that the woman's story does not end in hopelessness. In the letter she bore testimony to having come back to her heavenly Father and experienced his loving, healing forgiveness.

Years later now, she and the child's father are doing everything they can to build a strong Christian home. God has made the broken whole!

There is forgiveness in Jesus' name.

If Jesus by his blood can forgive me of my sins, then who am I to withhold forgiveness from my brother or sister? The most ungrateful thing you or I can do is to stubbornly refuse to forgive another person.

Friends are worth forgiving.
Family members are worth forgiving.
Church members are worth forgiving.
Sinners are worth forgiving.

5. CLEAN OUT THE WOUNDS

You must make sure to get out all the infection of resentment, bitterness, and hate. If there is any trace of these three left in the wound, the wound cannot heal. Ask Jesus to clean it all out of you.

As in Gary's case, this may mean going to the person whom you have had ill feelings toward and asking for his forgiveness. Whatever it takes to get it cleaned out, do it. The healing that you are going to experience is worth whatever it costs you.

6. THANK JESUS BECAUSE HE'S TOUCHING YOU WITH HIS LOVE AND HEALING POWER

At the conclusion of my talk at a singles' retreat on how to get our hurts healed, a young woman remained behind after everyone left. There she sat, sobbing. Responding to her cry, I and a couple of the retreat workers gathered around her. After what seemed like a long period of time, she screamed, "I hate my mother. I hate her!" This was followed by a long silence.

Then she began to sob all over again as if her heart

were breaking in two and groaned: "She never touched
me. I'm thirty-three years of age and she never touched
me, never held me, and never kissed me." Then she wailed,
"All my life my mother has withheld her love from
me." Led by the Spirit of the Lord I said, "Jesus' arms are
around you. He is holding you now. Loving you just
like you are. You are a loved person." Experiencing the
presence and love of Jesus, the transformed lady
witnessed: "For the first time I know that I am loved."
Thank you, Jesus, for the healing sunshine of your
love that flows into all our dark, lonely spots!

7. RELINQUISH YOUR PAST HURT INTO JESUS' HAND
Put all your hurt in his hands. Leave the person who
hurt you in God's hands. One of the things about
human nature is that when we are hurt, we want to hurt
back. Not only because we are hurting, but because
the one who caused the hurt doesn't seem to be hurting.
And that seems unfair.

There are some very important practical teachings in
Romans that we must put to practice in every hurting
situation. God's Word to us is this, *"Dear friends, never
avenge yourselves. Leave that to God, for he has said
that he will repay those who deserve it"* (Rom. 12:19, TLB).

Why does God tell us to let go of it and put it into his
hands? Because he desires to protect us. We are not
qualified to make fair judgments. But God, our Father, is
the perfect judge of all things. Trust him now. Lay it
in his hands and believe that he does all things well.

**Release it, and walk in the sunshine rather than in
the darkness of ill feelings.**

We need to put in God's loving hands not only the
injustices we've suffered, but all our sorrows and
griefs. There is a vivacious, dear lady named Edna
Clausius who started to attend our church this past year.

She has suffered a great deal of hurt and pain in her life. But her personality radiates the love and joy of the Lord. She is a beautiful person.

Edna is one of the many people who have joined New Hope Community Church in the past year. During a pastor's class, where we prepare people for membership, I opened the floor for questions. Someone asked what happens to babies who die without being baptized. My answer was that when Jesus Christ died on the cross, he provided for them in their innocence. Every baby that dies, baptized or unbaptized, I believe goes directly to heaven.

As I said this, I looked at Edna, and tears of joy were streaming down her face. For twenty-seven years she had lived with the pain and agony of believing that her unbaptized infant who had died was lost. This misconception had given her untold pain and suffering. But thanks be to Jesus, as I spoke about God's love and how Jesus took care of babies, God reached down inside Edna and healed this deep wound.

For the first time in twenty-seven years Edna could relinquish her little baby into the hands of a loving God who does all things well.

8. TAKE A POSITIVE ACTION

It's not by accident that the Bible says, *"Conquer evil by doing good"* (Rom. 12:21, TLB). To be free in your own spirit, do something good for the person who has hurt you. If it's impossible for the relationship to continue, then plant your positive seed by praying that good things will happen in the other person's life. It's impossible to give away positive feelings without experiencing healing in your own spirit.

My friend, I have been healed from all my hurts. I have been involved in the healing of the walking wounded. And my heart goes out to you this moment. I believe in the name of Jesus that you are going to rise up and be healed.

I love the chorus of this song, "Rise and Be Healed":

Rise and be healed in the name of Jesus;
Let faith arise in your soul.
Rise and be healed in the name of Jesus;
He will make you every whit whole!
Rise and be healed in the name of Jesus;
Let faith arise in your soul.
Rise and be healed in the name of Jesus;
He will make you every whit whole!
Rise, rise, rise in the name of Jesus![2]

[1]Jose Naroski, Narymar, Buenos Aires.
[2]RISE AND BE HEALED by Milton Bourgeois, © Copyright 1972 by
Crown-Royal Music. International copyright secured. All rights reserved.
Used by permission of The Benson Company, Inc., Nashville.

SEVEN
REBUILDING SELF-ESTEEM

Not in the clamor of the crowded street,
Not in the shouts and plaudits of the throng,
But in ourselves, our triumph and defeat.
—Longfellow

A man who had been ousted by a power-play from the chairmanship of the board of a large corporation wanted to know, "What do you do when your self-esteem has been shattered?" Like a lot of you, I can relate personally to his question.

All my life I had enjoyed receiving good vibrations from most of the people around me. I had been a successful student and honors graduate of college and seminary. In my pastorates I had gotten lots of strokes and love from people who helped to feed my feelings that I was a worthwhile person. But then in 1970 I was hit by a family breakup and, like Humpty Dumpty, tumbled off the wall and smashed into a million pieces. Nothing could have been more shattering to my self-esteem. Suddenly a lot of people who had looked up to me started looking down at me as if I were a hopeless failure. To tell you the truth, I felt horrible about myself as a person.

Had I not made a revolutionary discovery just prior

to going through the hell of a divorce, I think I would never have recovered. More than likely I would have spent the rest of my life engaging in self-flagellation. What was this discovery that was to be my lifesaver in the churning sea of failure? It was the discovery that: *God had a dream for my self-esteem.*

Nothing that has happened in your life changes God's dream for your self-esteem.

How do you feel about yourself? The way you think and feel about yourself as a person affects every relationship and action of your life. An individual who does not like himself is going to be unhappy in marriage regardless of whom he marries. A person who doesn't like himself is going to be unhappy in his job no matter what the job is. A lack of good feeling about yourself boxes you into being self-centered, simply because you are forced to keep thinking about your miserable self all the time instead of being free to consider the needs of others.

Jesus said, "Love your neighbor . . . as yourself" (Matt. 23:39, TLB).

Someone else has said: "If you don't love yourself, your neighbor is in big trouble."

Many people suffer from low self-esteem because of the scars they carry from their childhood. Unfortunately a lot of people grow up believing untruths about themselves. Majoring on minors they wipe themselves out. Having chosen a negative view of themselves instead of a positive view, they sell themselves short.

John's father was a demanding perfectionist. When John was growing up, no matter what he did he never felt that he pleased his father. The approval that he longed for was withheld. Instead of receiving compliments, he was the object of put-downs. These cutting words of his father stuck in his memory. "You dumb kid, can't you ever do anything right?"

The tragic truth is that John's father really did love him. In fact, out of the six children, John was the one for whom he had the most hopes and dreams. But the emotional hangups within the father never allowed him to communicate warmth, touching, or love to his son. What he communicated was that John could never quite measure up to his father's expectations, and because of this he deserved to be punished.

Years later as an adult, John is still suffering from a wounded self-esteem. Whenever John's performance at anything is not perfect, he sets out to punish himself psychologically. Oh, that John might learn about God's dream for his self-esteem.

Let me tell you about a man who has started learning about God's dream for his self-esteem. Sonny has spent a good part of the last twenty years in and out of mental institutions. At one time psychiatrists pronounced his mental illness as being incurable. During his life he has suffered immeasurable pain.

With a smile on his face he testified to me that he came to know Jesus Christ three years ago. Being fed positive healing teachings since then through my books and the ministry of New Hope, he is beginning to feel like a worthwhile person for the first time in his life. Gone is the overwhelming obsession to try to be something he isn't. Gone is the compulsion to run himself down. Because of Christ's presence, love, and inner healing, he feels good about himself as a person. For the first time Sonny is experiencing healthy feelings of self-worth and value.

Whatever one's past experience has been, just about everyone I know could use a healthy dose of self-love.

**You can get on the beam
with a healthy dose of self-esteem.**

God's dream for your self-esteem is threefold. First, that you will love and accept yourself; second, that you will forgive yourself; and third, that you will believe in yourself.

1. LOVE AND ACCEPT YOURSELF

SEE YOURSELF AS BEING WONDERFULLY MADE

Someone has said, "God did not create you for creation. But he created creation for you." What a tremendous thought. God made the heavens and the earth with all of its breathtaking beauty for you. He filled the waters with fish, the air with birds, the earth with plant life and animal life, and he said, "It's yours to master and enjoy." This should tell you how much God thinks of you, his choice creation.

Of all God's creation you are the top of the line. God made you in his own image, after his own likeness.

Think about how wonderfully God has created you and be thankful. I remember talking to an ear and throat specialist. I asked him how many parts there were to the human ear. His reply was that there were more than 100 parts. Then he offered this observation. He said, "Although I have spent twenty years specializing in the human ear, there is still a mystery about the inner ear that I do not understand." Only a master designer like God could create such a fantastic organ. And to think, the ear is just one of hundreds of fantastically made parts in the human body.

Lift your voice, give thanks to God for how marvelously and wonderfully he has put you together.

ACCEPT YOUR UNIQUENESS AND REFUSE
TO PLAY THE DESTRUCTIVE COMPARISON GAME

Self-comparison is the most common reason for self-rejection. Comparing ourselves with others and measuring ourselves by them are real downers. Listen to what the Bible says about this unhealthy comparison game. *"They measuring themselves by themselves, and comparing themselves among themselves, are not wise"* (2 Cor. 10:12, KJV).

To compare yourself with another person is not only unwise, it is stupid. Comparing myself with another will lead to one of two conclusions. Either I am better than he is or I am inferior to him. Either conclusion leads to a wrong attitude. If on the one hand I think that the other person is better, it gives me an inferiority complex and causes me to try to bring the other person down to my level. On the other hand, if I conclude that I am better, it will cause me to act in a snobbish, arrogant way toward the other person.

The Bible contains numerous illustrations of the fallacy of comparing oneself with another. Cain compared himself with Abel and became uncontrollably jealous. His jealousy lead to murder [Gen. 4:8]. Esau compared himself with Jacob and lived a life of terrible defeat [Gen. 27:41]. The gifted and able King Saul compared himself with David and reacted with bitter envy [1 Sam. 18:6-9].

Suppose you go to the doctor and after he has examined you, he rattles off some great big words that you don't understand. Then he takes his prescription pad and scribbles on it and gives you a sheet to take to the pharmacy. As you leave, you look at the prescription. The first problem is that you can't read his writing, and the second one is that you couldn't even begin to understand the long words that he scribbled there.

You get into your car and all the time you think, *Boy, he's smart and I must be awfully stupid.* You've just committed the self-destructive sin of comparison. I wonder how that doctor would get along trying to perform your job. Chances are that doctor, who had twenty years of schooling learning those big words,

would fail miserably at your job. The point is, it is
an unfair comparison. The truth is that every comparison
is an unfair comparison. You were not meant to be
someone else. God created you to be *you*.

Be the best you can be.

A man and his wife and four children were riding
together in the family car on a trip. The three oldest ones
were in the back, and the youngest, six-year-old Paul,
was seated up front with his parents. The father
suggested, "Why don't we play the 'What If?' game? If you
could be anything you wanted to be, what would you
be?"

The oldest girl's response was immediate. "I'd like
to be the Bionic Woman." In turn, each of the children
named some contemporary hero that he would like
to be—all except Paul, who said nothing. The father
asked, "Well, Paul, what would you like to be if you
could be anything?"

"I'd just be me."

"Why?" father asked.

"Because I like me."

The father observed that Paul was the happiest, the
most well-adjusted of his children. It is a very healthy
thing to accept and like yourself.

Do yourself a big favor.
Stop trying to be anyone else.
Accept yourself as being unique and be the best self
you can be.

MAKE THE DISCOVERY THAT
IT IS WHAT'S INSIDE THAT COUNTS
A few weeks ago on Sunday morning I asked all those
present who had something they did not like about their
physical appearance, something they would like to

change, to hold up their hands. Do you know it looked as if everyone held up his hand? Curly haired people want straight hair. And straight-haired people want curly hair. Short people want to be taller. Tall people want to be shorter. Women who are heavily endowed want to be less endowed. Women who are less endowed wish they were more endowed.

Self-esteem is so much more than your physical appearance. Self-worth is something more than what you can do. Feelings about yourself as a person come from deep within.

Several years ago, a balloon salesman was selling balloons on the streets of New York City. When business got a little slow, he would release a balloon. As it floated into the air, a fresh crowd of buyers would gather and his business would pick up for a few minutes.

He alternated the colors; first releasing a white one, then a red one, and later, a yellow one. After a while, a little Mexican boy tugged at his coat sleeve, looked the balloon salesman in the eye, and asked a penetrating question. "Mister, if you had a brown balloon, would it go up?"

The balloon salesman looked at the little boy and with compassion, wisdom, and understanding, said, "Son, it's what's inside those balloons that made them go up." The little boy was fortunate indeed to encounter a man who could see with more than just his eyes. *You see, it is what's inside you that will make you go up.*

Beauty comes from the inside out.
And Jesus specializes in making something beautiful out of our lives from the inside out.

One of our new Christians at New Hope Community Church, Billie Smith, shares how God has been transforming her from the inside out. "Before experiencing New Hope, my life was OK, but one ingredient

was missing that gives life some purpose. I kept looking
and looking, wondering what it was. When I accepted
Jesus Christ into my life, I found what I was missing.
Jesus has filled up that blank space in my life. One
thing that has happened to me this year is that, for the
first time, I feel like a grown woman. I've always
felt like a little girl—my mother's daughter—but this year
I've really grown and felt full contentment and wholeness
inside. Jesus was the ingredient that I needed to
reach maturity and feel good about myself as a woman.
Now I look forward, with Christ's help, to growing into
Christian maturity."

LOVE WHAT GOD LOVES
A contest was held and the children were urged to
write an essay on why they would like to meet the President of the United States. When the many essays
were written, the judges chose one written by a nine-
year-old girl who said, "It's not so much for myself
that I want to meet the President of the United States, but
for my grandmother." She went on to explain that
her grandmother had been in a concentration camp in
Germany during World War II and the greatest sight that
she had ever seen was when the Americans came
and liberated the camp. The grandmother's life-long
desire had been to meet the leader of the United States.

The nine-year-old winner and her grandmother did,
in fact, meet President Reagan. The president took them
into the Oval Office for a fifteen-minute visit. He
stated that he had also been in the second World War and
had "flown a desk." His job was to review the recom-
mendations of those soldiers who had been nominated
for the Congressional Medal of Honor. He remembered
one of those letters of recommendation in particular;
it had stuck in his mind to this day.

A B-29 fighter-bomber plane had been shot up badly
during a raid and its landing gear was destroyed.
Down in the belly of the aircraft was a place where the

gunner was stationed. It was at the very bottom of
the plane and in a very tight, small space, with just
enough room for a man to crawl down into it. Because
the plane had been shot up so badly, the gunner
was trapped in this hole. The captain of the plane didn't
know how he was going to land the plane and keep
the gunner alive.

As they got closer to England, the captain realized that
he was not going to make it back to the airstrip.
As he began to lose control of the plane, he commanded
the crew to bail out. The gunner was trapped and
had no way of climbing up out of the hole.

Just as the last man was ready to jump, he looked and
saw the captain taking off his parachute, then saw
him lean over into the gunner's hole, take the gunner's
hand and say, "Well, Sergeant, looks like you and I
are going to land this thing together."

This story is amazing. The Bible says "scarcely"—that
means hardly ever—will a human being give his life
willingly for another. But this captain did give up his life
for his comrade. As wonderful a thing as this was, I
know a story even greater than this one. *"But God
commendeth his love toward us, in that, while we were yet
sinners, Christ died for us"* (Rom. 5:8, KJV).

The fact is that God loves and accepts you just as you
are. Now, if God loves you with such an amazing,
unconditional, unstoppable love, who are you not to love
and accept yourself?

Accept God's love and love yourself.

2. FORGIVE YOURSELF

The other day I read a story about a minister who had
become depressed due to a very negative self-image.
He was a senior pastor of a large church and obviously
things were not going very well.

Feeling defeated, he entered the sanctuary, knelt at the

altar, and prayed a very negative prayer. "O God, I am nothing. I am a worm. I can't do anything right." Over and over he repeated these degrading words.

As he was praying, his associate pastor walked by and was very impressed by what his senior minister was praying. So he went and joined him and prayed the same kind of prayer. "O Lord, I am nothing. I am a worm. I can't do anything right."

While the two ministers were praying, the janitor happened to walk by and overheard them. Not to be outdone, he, too, knelt at the altar and said, "O Lord, I, too, am nothing. I am a worm. I can't do anything right."

Just then the associate minister stopped praying, looked over at the janitor, then turned to the senior pastor and said, "What's he doing up here praying like us. Who does he think he is anyway?"

I chuckled when I heard this anecdote. I also felt like crying because too many sincere people live by this kind of false humility, which is nothing more than self-humiliation.

It is disturbing to realize how many people engage in self-flagellation. It is even more tragic to see large numbers of Christian people who think they have to keep on punishing themselves. You can't imagine how good it feels when you come to the place you can stop beating and berating yourself.

EXPERIENCE THESE WORDS: "I AM FORGIVEN"
Nothing cuts away at the foundation of your self-esteem like sin and guilt. When you're feeling guilty, it is very difficult to love others. To love requires you to reveal yourself, and when you're feeling guilty you are afraid to share very much of yourself because you do not want to be found out. To the guilty, there is always the fear of exposure. "If they knew what I've done, they

wouldn't have anything to do with me." Guilt keeps us from loving others and it causes us to hate ourselves.

How can we wilt our guilt and disclaim our shame?

My friend, there is nothing like forgiveness to make a heart sing and a soul rejoice again. There is only one kind of sin that God cannot forgive and that is unconfessed sin. Right now, where you are, open up your sins to the Lord. Confess them and even as you do, the forgiveness of Jesus will flow into your life.

I love this song that my wife, Margi, sings:

I am forgiven by His blood,
His sacrifice of love.
So completely it applies to my need
I failed Him—forsook Him
But He understood.
He forgave me—now I am redeemed!
You are forgiven! Forgiven! Forgiven!
Forgiven today.[1]

I think three of the most beautiful words in all the world are these. "I am forgiven."

Too many people become their own judge, jury, and prosecution, continuing to inflict blow upon blow of self-condemnation on themselves. Nothing drags down one's self-love more than a depressing recall of shameful deeds or failure. It serves no good to keep going over past mistakes. It is a burden too large for any one person to bear. It can result in mental strain, nervousness, and acute anxiety. It will destroy your confidence.

Believe that Christ Jesus took upon himself all your punishment when he died upon the cross. Accept it and be thankful. God has forgiven you. Now, forgive yourself.

RETHINK THE WAY YOU THINK ABOUT YOURSELF
Stop thinking about yourself as a guilty sinner, and start thinking about yourself as a forgiven child of God.

The man wanted to know, "What do you do when your past sins keep coming up in your mind after you've asked the Lord to forgive you?" I'll tell you what you do—you use your God-given willpower to discipline your own mind. Now, many times you can't stop a thought from coming into your mind, but you can take action to get it out of your mind. Once you've asked God to forgive you, claim that forgiveness, and from that point on, refuse to allow any condemnation to take over in your thought life. Refuse to be wiped out by sins that Christ has already forgiven in your life.

Affirm right now this wonderful truth: Christ lives within me, so I am a wonderful person. Christ has forgiven me, so I will forgive myself. Say it! I AM FORGIVEN.

NOT PERFECT, BUT LEARNING
In April 1977, I made a mistake that I am still paying for. At that time I purchased a '77 Monte Carlo that I thought was a black beauty. I was soon to discover that my black beauty on six out of the seven days in a week turned into my dirty bird. The hard lesson I learned is that a black car is the most difficult to keep clean.

My usual practice is to get it washed on Saturdays so it will look nice on Sundays. After all, when I am preaching every Sunday and people are gathering in their cars, I can't arrive in a dirty-bird car. I want to put my best foot forward and have it looking shiny and clean.

A couple Saturdays ago I was out running some errands, so I thought I would run my black car through the car wash. I pulled into the Rub-A-Dub Car Wash to get the job done. The moment I reached into my back

pocket to get my billfold out to pay the attendant,
I remembered that my billfold was in my briefcase which
was in the trunk. Then when I searched on my key
ring for the trunk key, I discovered it was missing. The
result was that I had to go home with a dirty car.

As I pulled into the driveway, Margi was just finishing
washing the car that someone had loaned her to drive.
After I told her what had happened to me, she said,
"Why don't you just wash your car here?"

I said, "That's what I will do after supper." And I went
on inside to relax.

Our four-year-old Scott overheard the conversation
between Margi and me. The little guy followed me into
the house and announced that he would wash the car.
Knowing that there wasn't anything to lose, I said
OK. Scott got a rag and went outside, turned on the hose,
and went to work.

After quite a while Scott came back in all smiles. He
was really pleased with himself. I said, "Did you do
a good job?"

He gave me a big smile and said, "Yep."

About this time Margi said, "Dale, come here. You've
got to see your car." I wish you could have seen it.
My dirty-bird car had turned into a streaker. I mean there
were streaks all over it. Large areas of untouched
dirt remained, half clean and half unclean.

There was no way in an adult world that I could leave
my car looking like that. As an adult you would look
at it and say, "That's completely unacceptable." But for a
four-year-old, Scott did a tremendous job. *Not perfect—
but learning.*

Start to be realistic with yourself. Nobody is perfect!
No person who thinks about it could really expect
anyone to be perfect. People will not reject you simply
because you're not perfect. So why should you reject
yourself because there are some imperfections in your
life?

Often self-hate has it roots in childhood. Once a man

told me how he and his wife were enjoying a leisurely breakfast in bed one morning when he upset the coffee. He found himself exploding. "I hate myself when I do that!" he said aloud. His wife helped him clean it up. Being a very calm person, she asked him what was the big deal. Everybody spills something at sometime.

As he analyzed it, he remembered that in his childhood whenever he spilled something at the table as children do, his father would rant and rave at him and rub his face in what he had spilled. Parents take note: children should never be punished for accidents. They should be taught how to avoid accidents but never be punished for them.

Everyone has weaknesses. Let's say your weakness is that you have a short fuse. You have a temper. Because you have a hot temper, does that mean that you are not acceptable as a person? Does it mean that you are not a Christian? No! It simply means that you have an area of your life that, with Christ's help, you need to work on. Being a Christian often includes following an improvement program.

How patient God is with us! I am so glad that he's not finished with me yet. As his children, we are in the process of becoming. We have not yet arrived. The promise is: *He that has begun a good work within us will complete it* (See Phil. 1:6). Someone has said if you don't like yourself, simply get back up on God's easel and let him finish the job.

There are two things you can do when you make a mistake. You can feel sorry for yourself and give up, or you can learn. Being a follower of Jesus Christ means being a learner. The wonderful thing is that while we are in the process of learning, God the Father helps us, accepts us, forgives us, strengthens us, picks us up, and keeps on teaching us how to become.

Affirm these truths from the Word of God and feel good about yourself:

I am forgiven (See Luke 5:20).

There's no condemnation to those who are in Christ Jesus (See Rom. 8:1).

I am a new person in Christ (2 Cor. 5:17-21).

I am becoming (See Phil. 1:6).

I can do all things through Christ who strengthens me (Phil. 4:13).

3. BELIEVE IN YOURSELF
Did you know that it is easier to believe in God than it is to believe in yourself? If I were to speak to each of you personally and ask, "Do you believe in God?" ninety-nine percent, perhaps everyone, would say, "Yes." Then if I asked, "Do you believe in yourself?" a lot of you would have difficulty saying yes.

Millions of people suffer from a lack of self-confidence. Thousands of people think of themselves as inferior. They are full of fear and do not believe in themselves. Self-doubt, which is actually fear, can hold you back when you could be moving ahead.

Right now I want to share with you a basic secret for a satisfying and successful life. Here it is: *Believe in God and believe in yourself.* In Mark 5:36, we read, *"Be not afraid, only believe."*

The Bible stresses the importance of self-confidence when it says: *"In quietness and in confidence shall be your strength"* (Isa. 30:15, KJV).

BELIEVE THAT YOU ARE A CHILD OF GOD
The first step for you to take in developing self-confidence is to discover who you are. Who are you? An accident? A nobody? A hopeless sinner? No! You are a choice person who was created by God to be his child.

I want you to discover what a wonderful person you

really are and can become. No matter what has happened in your life, no matter how inferior you may think yourself, God wants you to accept your rightful sonship. Why be a nobody when you can be a somebody? The Bible says, *"As many as received him, to them gave he power to become the sons of God, even to them that believe on his name"* (John 1:12, KJV).

Do you know what it means to be a child of God? It means that you are loved, you are forgiven. You're not on this earth just by chance, but your life has a purpose. You have been elected, chosen by God to be his child.

Unfortunately many people going through the motions of being God's children have yet to feel inside the confidence that comes from being a child of God.

I want you to feel deep down inside what it means to be a child of God. It means that for you, all things are possible with God. It means that you can do all things through Christ who strengthens you. It means that you are in the process of becoming.

As someone has said, "God got you started, God has helped you get where you are, and you can be sure that God will not quit on you. Just make doubly sure that you never quit on God."

GIVE A LIFT TO YOURSELF
BY COMMITTING YOURSELF TO A GREAT CAUSE
One thing that has given my life a continuing lift since I was fifteen years of age has been my firm commitment to the world's greatest cause. Do you know what the world's greatest cause is? It is the cause of Jesus Christ. *I am proud of the gospel of Christ; for it is the power of God unto salvation to everyone that believes* [See Rom. 1:6].

Commit yourself to a cause worth living for. Get out of the grandstand and on to the playing field. Move into the spotlight of creative and constructive involvement. Run the race and you will win the prize.

The story is told of two mountain men who sat on a log looking dreamily across the valley to a distant mountain range. One mountaineer was a huge man; the other was a small man. The following conversation took place between the little man (L.M.) and the big man (B.M.)

L.M.: I'll bet there's big bear in them thar hills.
B.M.: Uh-huh.
L.M.: I wish I was a big man like you. You know what I'd do if I was a big man like you?
B.M.: Uh-uh.
L.M.: I'd go into them thar hills and catch me a big bear and I'd tear him limb from limb! That's what I'd do if I was a big man like you!
B.M.: (turning to face little man) There's plenty of little bear in them hills, too!

Do what you can do and stop talking about what you can't do. The greatest feeling in all the world is to know that God is using your life. Finding and following God's plan for your life is the surest, soundest way to self-confidence. Make these words your theme: *"I can do all things through Christ that strengtheneth me"* (Phil. 4:13, KJV).

[1]YOU ARE FORGIVEN by Rich Cook, © Copyright 1976 by John T. Benson Publishing Co. International copyright secured. All rights reserved. Used by permission of The Benson Company, Inc., Nashville.

E I G H T
BITTER OR BETTER—
THE CHOICE IS YOURS!

*Let the words of my mouth and the meditation of my
heart be acceptable in thy sight, O Lord, my strength
and my redeemer* (Psa. 19:14, KJV).

Someone you trusted has just cheated you out of a large
sum of money.

Bitter or better—the choice is yours!

You have just discovered that your mate is having an
affair.

Bitter or better—the choice is yours!

The other person got the promotion and raise that you
deserved.

Bitter or better—the choice is yours!

Your only daughter has been raped and murdered by a
motorcycle gang.

Bitter or better—the choice is yours!

You have been unfairly criticized while trying to do your best.

Bitter or better—the choice is yours!

Your children have continually disappointed you.

Bitter or better—the choice is yours!

You have suffered an ego-deflating setback in your business.

Bitter or better—the choice is yours!

It seems that the harder you try, the more things go wrong.

Bitter or better—the choice is yours!

Peggy was going through a divorce that was tearing her apart emotionally. She had been the innocent victim of severe physical and psychological abuse administered by her husband. The process of divorce was heightening his abusiveness. With a smile on her face, Peggy taught me an important lesson that I want to share with you. She said God was teaching her that no matter how much she was hurting at the moment, in the final outcome whether her ordeal would make her bitter or better was her choice. Then she added, "With God's help I will become better—not bitter!" Two years later I saw her again and I can tell you that out of her pain has come great gain. She is an altogether beautiful person.

Sooner or later unjust, painful blows are suffered by

all of us, for whoever said that life was fair? When
it happens to you, you will never be the same person
again. Afterward you will either be bitter or better—the
choice is yours.

**No matter what happens to you you have the important
attitude choice.
The attitude you choose will either make you bitter
or better.**

THE CHOICE IS YOURS

Eight-year-old Tommie was bragging to his dad about
what a great hitter he was becoming. His dad took
him out in the backyard to give him an opportunity to
demonstrate his newfound hitting ability. When they
got in the backyard, Tommie's dad said, "Go ahead and
show me what you can do." With a confident grin,
Tommie threw the ball in the air, swung at it, and missed.
"Strike one," said his dad. Knowing he could hit
the ball, Tommie threw it in the air again, and missed.
"Strike two," laughed his father. And again, "Strike three."

Not to be beaten, Tommie said, "Boy, am I a great
pitcher."

No matter what happens to you, you still have a choice.
There is no such thing as a choiceless life. You *always*
have a choice! For example, suppose someone does
something that has hurt you. What has happened is
external, outside of you. Your reaction that takes place on
the inside is your own. You respond, "But I can't do
anything about what has happened to me." Right
there you have given up without a fight. You can do
something. Your reaction to what has happened is still
your own choice. How you choose to react is the one
thing that no one can take away from you.

In the past seven years since my first book was

published in 1975, I have received hundreds of letters from people whose hearts have been broken by the tragedy of divorce. Besides this, I have personally counseled hundreds of other people. Two of these are representative of the opposite ways people react to the same personal crisis.

Five years ago, a man whom we will call Bill Brown had the shattering experience of having his wife run off with another man, never to return. At the time this happened, he had a very successful business.

Five years later now, if you were to talk with him personally, before long you would hear him blaming the failure of his business on this horrible, sinful woman who deserted him. He keeps rehearsing the hurt over and over and over. He is playing a broken record and that keeps him broken apart. He angrily verbalizes wanting to kill his ex-wife and her lover. Five years after the fact, he is a bitter defeated man.

The other day I had in my office a young lady named Bernice. Five months ago Bernice's husband left her to move in with his secretary. In a few days the divorce will be final. Bernice loved her husband and has shed many a painful tear over what has happened. But because she has already forgiven her husband, Bernice is free in her spirit. She is facing the future, believing that somehow, some way, with God's help, she will rebuild her life. She is getting better because her spirit is free from ill feelings.

What's the difference between these two persons? The man has been divorced for five years and he is still hurting, hurting. And he will be hurting five years from now unless he deals with his bitterness and changes his attitude. On the other hand, Bernice is healing after just five months and she already is becoming a more beautiful, better person through this crisis. What makes the difference? The difference comes from the choice of attitude.

More important than what the other person has done or not done. More important than what has happened to you. More important than your circumstance. More important than fact or feeling.

MORE IMPORTANT THAN ANYTHING ELSE IS THE CHOICE OF YOUR OWN ATTITUDE. YOU HAVE A CHOICE —THE BITTER WAY OR THE BETTER WAY.

THE BITTER CHOICE

Certainly no one wants to hurt. As you may know, emotional pain can be more intense and excruciating than any physical suffering. From reading my book thus far, you know that I know what it is to be hurt emotionally. I understand that when you're hurting, no matter what the cause, you hurt.

To be honest, I don't like to hurt. Because I feel compassion for you, I want to save you all the pain I can. Thus I must warn you here and now that there is a disease that can get into our emotional wounds and bring far more excruciating pain to us than any hurt another party can inflict upon us. What is this enemy that would attack our very soul and make us go on suffering long after we should have been healed? It is the destructive disease of bitterness.

Whenever you have been hurt, that wound is open to the attack of bitterness. The Bible says, *"Watch out that no bitterness takes root among you, for as it springs up it causes deep trouble, hurting many in their spiritual lives"* (Heb. 12:15, TLB).

Bitterness can make you sick. Doctors bear testimony that 75-80 percent of the patients they see are physically ill not because of a disease but because of dis-ease of mind. And their dis-ease of mind is caused by bad feelings that they have toward another person. It is a proven fact that the bad chemistry of negative feelings produces both symptoms of physical illness and physical illness itself. Whenever we allow our minds to become preoccupied with hurts and dwell on what a dirty deal we've gotten, we are making ourselves sick.

My friend, Dr. David L. Messenger, in his book, *Dr. Messenger's Guide to Better Health* (Fleming H. Revell Co., 1981) relates a story about a patient with high blood pressure and ulcers who came to see him. The man could not sleep at night. His problem centered in a broken relationship with a former employer. According to the man's bitter testimony, the former boss had promised him a significant salary increase along with generous benefits that included a partnership in the company. Although this man faithfully served his employer and did his job well, none of these promises ever materialized. The man's pride was hurt and his spirit was wounded. Into that wounded spirit came the more destructive germ of bitterness. Dr. Messenger said that the patient's physical symptoms were all manifestations of this deep hurt, mixed with bitterness.

Dr. Messenger pointed out to his patient that he was making himself sick. He was the one who had high blood pressure, the beginnings of an ulcer, and couldn't sleep at night, while his boss was not hurting at all. The doctor prescribed for the hurting, wounded man a cleansing of his spirit from bitterness.

Sick or well.
Bitter or better.
The choice is yours.

Bitterness can turn your friends into enemies. King Saul's closest friend was David. They enjoyed many hours of close comradeship together. But over petty jealousies and hurts, Saul allowed bitterness to creep in and capture his thoughts and eat away at his spirit. We see him turning on his friend, David, and seeking to kill him. In the end, the most powerful man in Israel, the king, came tumbling down. He had destroyed himself because of the destructive disease of bitterness. In seeking to wipe out another person, he only succeeded in wiping out himself.

Bitterness can make you repulsive without your even knowing it, to the point that other people will not want to be around you.

Once in a while in order to be alone and have a chance to really communicate with one another, Margi and I will get into the car and go for a drive. One of the things we like to do is to look at new homes. On one such day, a fall afternoon, we stopped at the home of a builder whose homes we had viewed before. He really is a fine builder of quality homes.

Having made the dream tour of the home, we were about to get back into our car when Margi suggested that we go and look at the home next door by another builder. I said, "OK, why not?"

We were met at the front door by the builder who was an eager seller. He was most anxious to give us the grand tour in person. But instead of majoring on the good points of his house, he seized the opportunity to tell us all the things that were wrong with the house next door, where we had just been. It became so evident that he hated the builder next door. Through our entire tour he poured out the venom of his bitterness over a business deal he'd had with this builder. He called the man a cheat and a thief, and warned us that if we bought a house from him we'd be sorry.

What could have been a nice experience turned into a bad experience. We were so glad to get out of that house and back into our car. He followed us all the way to the car, still bad-mouthing the man next door. As I backed out of the driveway, he was still standing there cursing the man.

Now if Margi and I were in the market for a new house, do you think we would go back and talk to the bitter

man? Not on your life! Between you and me, I don't care
if I ever see the man again. Visiting with him was
anything but an inviting, pleasant experience. One thing
about bitterness, it's like an uncontrollable jack-in-
the-box, always popping up when you don't want it.

Here are three things you can do to clean out any and
all bitterness,

1. LEAVE ALL VENGEANCE TO THE LORD

In the Bible we read these words, *"Dear friends, never
avenge yourselves, leave that to God, for he has said
that he will repay those who deserve it. Don't take the law
into your own hands"* (Rom. 12:19, TLB). THERE ARE
A LOT OF THINGS THAT CAN HAPPEN IN LIFE THAT
YOU JUST HAVE TO LEAVE TO GOD.

2. PRACTICE FORGIVENESS

There is no healing without forgiveness. Without forgiveness, there is only hurt made worse by infection.
Forgiveness is your answer. Follow your Lord's example.
"Father, forgive these people," Jesus said, *"for they
don't know what they are doing"* (Luke 23:34, TLB).

3. DRAW CLOSE TO GOD—AND DRAIN OUT NEGATIVE EMOTIONS

I recently had some very negative feelings toward a
person who I felt had been attacking me unjustly. This
person had destroyed his wife emotionally and was
in the process of destroying his children. He had made a
mess of his own life. His comments about me were
very cruel when he did not even know what he was
talking about.

I took it to the Lord in prayer and drained out all of
the negative feelings. I realized that I was responsible for
my own reaction; I was not responsible for what the
other man said or did. As I prayed, I got free in my spirit,
and love and understanding began to flow into my

heart toward this man. I began to see that all of his life he had felt unloved and insecure. The next time I met the man I was able to show love to him.

**Talking to God honestly works miracles.
Open up to God and he opens up heaven to you.
He renews the right spirit within you.**

For a long time I've wondered how it is that so many people say they have forgiven and yet they don't seem to be free in their spirits. Just the other day I got this new insight from the Lord and I share it with you. We haven't really, completely forgiven the other person until we come to a point where we wish and we pray for good things to happen to that person. If we are secretly wishing the other person harm, then it is evident that we've not yet completely forgiven.

Forgiveness holds nothing in reserve but lets go of all ill feelings and replaces ill feelings with the positive feeling of love and good will.

THE BETTER CHOICE
Recently in our television mail we received a letter from a blind lady. First of all, I was fascinated to realize that a blind person was tuning into our television program and enjoying it so much. The dear lady, after commenting how much the program had helped her, shared the following:

I am twice a widow—once from cancer and the second time by a drowning on our honeymoon. It is my opinion that we were not meant to travel through this life alone— otherwise we would have been created differently. I was born blind but have conquered that rather amply in that I have always held a good job and lived independently

in my own home and feel very normal. But this widowhood
is yet another thing. I enjoy being married and having
companionship and going home to prepare a meal.

My thought in writing is that you might pray for me that
someone can be sent to me. My petition seems to go
unheeded, and it cannot be that God would wish me to be
the rest of my days alone.

My attitudes are not in the 'poor me' theme as I feel
blessed with health, family and friends, job, home and all
those assets.

This yearning is within me at other times of the year
but it seems acute around Christmas time. Please include
me in your prayer petition.

Then she explained that rather than our writing her,
she would appreciate a phone call.

When one of our beautiful television workers, Ruth
Steenson, called this woman, she received the good word
that the prayer was already being answered.

Now here was a person who had known physical
handicap. Setbacks. Tragedies. And yet, because she had
chosen the better attitude, she was winning the victory.
And though admittedly her life was not without
problems, she was, with God's help, finding solutions to
her problems. Now, the things that happened in this
woman's life would have wiped out a lot of us. But not
her, because she exercised the right choice again
and again and chose the better attitude.

So did a member of our church named Carol Patzer. I
confess to you that I admire Carol. She is a teacher
in specialized education in the Portland public school
system. Compassionately, she gives herself to these
special children. Every Sunday I see her at church with
several special foster children to whom she gives
a home. She treats these handicapped children with a
rare combination of toughness and tenderness. As if she
didn't have enough to do, she teaches children in
Sunday school.

It's been only three years since Carol lost her husband. I want you to read her testimony written in her own words of how she faced this personal crisis.

The sun was so bright and warm, making a beautiful day at the beach March 19, 1979. It was a special time for my husband and me to be alone on our twelfth anniversary "honeymoon." Suddenly, like a fierce storm striking, my husband said, "My ticker feels funny." He went into the bathroom, where instantly he passed out and died of a heart attack while I watched helplessly.

That first Sunday back at New Hope after the funeral was a difficult one for me. I'll never forget the lady sitting next to me, who was a total stranger. She sensed my need and put her arm around me, which made me feel like she cared. Then I heard Margi Galloway sing, "Because He Lives." Those words sounded so beautiful! "Because He lives, I can face tomorrow, Because He lives, all fear is gone, Because I know He holds the future, And life is worth the living just because He lives."[1] It made the tears come but it was good for me. Then I heard Pastor Galloway pray for me and my family during prayer time. When I thought of the hundreds of people attending with big needs, it made me feel new strength and comfort to know they asked God's help for me. And that help came in marvelous ways—like friends concerned over my leaky roof and car problems.

I had visited New Hope only a few times before this dramatic experience in my life, so it really touched me to have the help God sent to cope with loss of my husband. At New Hope, God helped me learn to be thankful for the twelve years of having my husband. I learned the positive attitude that brings gain through pain and encourages having new dreams and goals which bring healing.

I knew I had a choice to become a bitter person and withdraw into self-pity or to be a better person because of my loss and to let God use my life to reach out to others

*and show his love. I thank and praise God that I can share
in the ministry of New Hope so I can become a better
person.*

My friend, whatever has happened in your life, you, too,
with God's help, can become a better person.

NINE
DOVE OR PIGEON?

We can make our plans, but the final outcome is in God's hands (Prov. 16:1, TLB).

A SIGN FROM GOD?
After four years of holding our church services in everything from a day-care center equipped with jungle gyms to a drive-in theater, we were beginning to feel like the children of Israel in their wanderings in the wilderness. We were getting anxious to have our own church home.

Our possibility-thinking church leaders had hammered out high standards by which they would evaluate any prospective piece of property. It had been our prayer and desire that we would not get into any property that would in any way hamper our ability to reach the unchurched thousands of the Portland metropolitan area. We were not looking for just any piece of property but the most choice acreage upon which to build. Our criteria were that it had to be close to a major free-way, within fifteen minutes of 100,000 people, a highly visible location, and one of inspiring natural beauty.

Across the years we explored and examined many different properties. On several occasions we even tried to purchase, but for one reason or another, nothing had worked out.

Then, on Tuesday, July 13, 1976, Carl Meyer, a fine Christian realtor, took me to see an eighteen-acre site located on Sunnyside Road, one mile off the Sunnyside exit of Freeway I-205.

Immediately I fell in love with this beautiful hillside property. I began to dream and visualize. The next day our board of directors decided that this piece of property fit all of our standards, and we voted unanimously to purchase it.

Early Friday morning, July 16, I phoned my good friends Pastor Rich Kraljev and Phil DeFresne and invited them to hike with me to the top of what we were already calling our "Promised Land." It was a long, hard climb to the top. Kidding, I told these two husky men that I had chosen them from all the others because I knew that if I had a heart attack climbing "cardiac hill," they could carry me out.

When the three of us reached the top and stood there amidst the tall fir trees, we looked out for miles over the city below. It was a breathtaking experience. We exclaimed, "Only God could make this kind of beauty!"

After we made it back to the flatland at the front of the property, we sat down to catch our breath. In wonder we looked back up the hillside from which we'd come. There, close to the top of the hill in a giant fir tree that towered majestically above everything else, we saw something that sent shivers up and down our spines. We saw something that I have never seen before or since in the twelve years I've lived in Oregon.

There in the tip-top of the huge tree was perched a pure snow-white dove. It sat there quietly, not moving, as if in that holy moment it had been placed there by God himself.

In the Bible we read about a dove appearing at the

baptism of Jesus as a sign from God that he was well pleased with his beloved Son. In the Old Testament we read that Noah sent a dove out from the ark to see if God was ready for them to find dry land. And, when the dove returned with an olive branch in its mouth, it was a sign from God that their wait was over.

Whenever the dove appears in the Bible, it is a sign from God that he is present and he is giving his approval.

If there is one thing we've wanted in the ministry of New Hope Community Church, beginning from day one and continuing through thick and thin, it has been that we would do exactly what God wanted us to do.

Once our people saw this property, it did not take long for them to get excited. What we needed was $23,000 in cash for a down payment toward the purchase price of $79,000, with the balance to be carried on a contract. Considering the small number of people we had at that time and their limited financial resources, raising $23,000 within ninety days looked not only impossible but ridiculous.

The New Hope people responded wholeheartedly to the challenge. They dug down deep and came up with sacrificial seed-faith gifts. And when all the contributions were totaled up, we had our $23,000 for a down payment on what we believed to be our "Promised Land."

A HARD BLOW THAT WE COULD NOT UNDERSTAND

Have you ever had something happen to you that you couldn't understand? I mean, you had faith, you did everything you thought was right, you plunged ahead in believing faith, and all of a sudden nothing is worked out right? And you began to ask, "Where is God in all this? I mean, I thought he was with me, but where did he go?"

Believing from our hearts that the Sunnyside property

was our "Promised Land," we hired an architect
and began to put our dream on paper. As a part of our
preparation for building, we made application to
Clackamas County for a conditional use zoning for a
church.

To our utter surprise and chagrin, unfriendly neighbors
showed up at the hearing and opposed our application.
Until this time, I had never heard of neighbors being
against something good like a church. But that's exactly
what happened. At the Planning Commission hearing
on September 27, 1976, ten neighbors, having been stirred
up by an agitator, vocalized strong objections to any
approval of our conditional use zoning. However, because
we met all the requirements legally for a conditional
use zoning for a church and were planning a beautiful
project, the Planning Commission approved our application anyhow.

A few days later, the same stirred-up neighbors
appealed to the county commission, and as irrational as
it seemed, the commissioners chose to reverse the
Planning Commission's decision and deny our conditional use.

My heart was broken. I was so disappointed and
bewildered by this unjust decision that I actually became
physically ill for a couple of weeks. Where was God
in all this?

I finally remembered that nowhere in the Bible does
God promise that doing his will or accomplishing his
purposes on this earth will be easy. In fact, one thing God
had been teaching me was that the greater the thing
you try to do for God, the more obstacles and opposition
you can expect.

We decided to stand and fight for what we thought
was right. We had our attorney make a legal appeal
through the court process. Being one of the finest
attorneys in the state of Oregon, he made an appeal
that had every promise of winning. Yet, without even

giving the case a fair hearing, the judge went against us.

Not to be denied, nine months later we petitioned Clackamas County a second time to let us use this property for a church. This time we did not even get to first base before being turned down. As a reason for turning us down, the hearing office wrote, "It is my opinion that New Hope Community Church will put too much traffic on Sunnyside Road." The interesting thing is that Sunnyside Road is a main artery into the freeway system. Later the Clackamas County planners would increase the density on this same property to allow for 180 condo units.

This was a very difficult time for me. I did not understand what was happening. I had felt so strongly that this was the property on which God wanted us to build his church.

About this time, jokingly, our board of directors began to ask me if it were not true that I had mistakenly thought I saw a dove when all the time it had been a pigeon. What about it, had I misread the sign? Had my eyes played a trick? Had it been a pigeon or a dove?

I HATE TO WAIT
Just yesterday afternoon I went to lunch to one of my favorite luncheon spots. The line of people waiting to get in was backed up outside the front door. I took one look at the line and concluded, "I'm not going to wait." I left. I am not the only one who hates to wait. Waiting is one of our least popular pastimes. Right at the top with death and taxes. Let's get a little more personal. How do you like to wait? Just as I thought, you don't like to wait either.

A desperate man in a pleading voice wanted to know, "Why doesn't God answer my prayer? It says in the Bible, *'Ask and it shall be given you'* (Matt. 7:7, KJV). I've prayed, I've pleaded, I've begged, and still nothing happens." Then he added, "Doesn't he care about what's happening to me?"

This desperate man was me.

During this most frustrating period of time, I learned this priceless lesson:

Sometimes God says: "Wait."

For some reason God works on a different timetable than we do. Noah waited 120 years before it rained. Job suffered long and hard before he finally triumphed over his tragedy. Jesus waited thirty years before he began his public ministry.

Our problem is that we are so programmed to want to see results instantly. We want it to happen right now! The only things that grow so fast are toadstools. It takes a long time to grow an oak tree. The waiting time is preparation time for something greater that is yet to come.

When you grow weary and tired of waiting, remember this promise: *"And let us not get tired of doing what is right, for after a while we will reap a harvest of blessing if we don't get discouraged and give up"* (Gal. 6:9, TLB).

During this time of being frustrated because nothing seemed to be moving ahead, I learned that:

God's delays are not God's denials.
God's delays are guidelines to greater things to come.

Be patient. God is working everything out. At the right time, in the right way, everything will evolve beautifully. What you and I need to do is keep on keeping on doing our best and leaving the timing and the outcome to God.

To think, all the time I could see only what looked like the end of the road, we were just at a bend in the road. All the days and months I was frustrated and struggling over this property deal, God was saying, "Wait. I have something better for the ministry of New Hope." Without the setbacks and delays of the Sunnyside Road property experience, we would not have been prepared for what God had for us in the days to come.

SOMETHING MORE
THAN THE SUNNYSIDE ROAD PROPERTY

A closer look at the Sunnyside Road property revealed some built-in growth restrictive problems that we had not seen at first. We discovered that because of the rough terrain a large percentage of the property was undevelopable. And the part that wasn't would be extremely costly to develop.

To fulfill the vast lifetime dream of multiple ministries of new hope, to heal the hurts and build the dreams of unchurched thousands, we had to have the best of locations. Once I got my vision up out of the mire of self-pity and started looking for something greater, a marvelous miracle began to happen.

No matter where I drove in this large metropolitan area I kept coming back to and focusing on the Sunnyside exit off Freeway I-205. This was the hot spot. Right in the center of the next twenty years of explosive development.

All my attention and dreams began to focus on a lush, green, gentle sloping, hillside located along the freeway directly across from where the largest shopping center in Oregon would soon be constructed.

Our investigation into the property revealed that because of its high density zoning, its value was close to a million dollars. One of the top realtors in the area said, "There's no way you will ever get the owners of that property to sell it to you for a church. They're not going to sell it for anything except apartments or condominiums."

God never closes one door without opening another.

At this time God brought some new friends, Don and Elva Ford, into our lives and into the ministry of New Hope. Don had completed a lovely, custom-built home just two blocks from the prospective property. One day Elva came to see me at the office and told me this beautiful house had been on the market for six months and no one had bought it. Then she informed me that she believed this would be an ideal home for us. To please her, Margi and I went to look at the house. We loved the house but knew it was a dream beyond anything we could afford at that time. But it didn't cost anything to dream, so we enjoyed going through the whole house.

I told Elva that we loved the house but could not afford it. She kept telling me that she believed this was the house God wanted us to have. One morning I woke up early with an idea of how we could move into this dream house. If the Fords would agree to take a second note for two years, we could do it. I made the proposal to them and they accepted. Within a few weeks the home we were living in sold and we packed up our family and moved into our dream house. In the two years that followed, we used our spacious living room for pastor's classes, Bible studies, board meetings, and a host of other special activities that could not have been carried on otherwise. We literally wore out our front room rug.

In God's perfect plan, I now drove by the million dollar piece of property every day. And every day I dreamed of what a perfect location this would make to reach the unchurched thousands. I mean it had it all—visibility, accessibility, developability, inspiring natural beauty.

HOW DO YOU BUY A MILLION DOLLAR PROPERTY WITHOUT ANY MONEY?

As soon as I got my own faith level up to the point where I believed we could claim this property, I began to

lead our lay leaders and people into claiming it with me.
We concluded that nowhere could there be a more
choice, prime, inspiring property than this one. I knew
from my research that the three interrelated parcels
of land that we were trusting and asking God for either
belonged to or were controlled by the Rawlins family.
I also knew that these people were sophisticated real
estate investors who lived in Salem. I prayed and asked
God to show me how to make contact with these owners.

In a few days, in January 1978, I received a phone
call inviting me to be the guest speaker at a Valentine's
banquet in a church in Salem. At the Valentine's banquet
Margi and I sat right next to the master of ceremonies,
who was Dwayne Rawlins. We had a delightful evening
and enjoyed much good Christian fellowship with
Dwayne and his wife. Dwayne shared with me how he
had been using my books to teach various classes in their
church. That evening I had no idea that Dwayne
Rawlins was a member of the Rawlins family who owned
the land we were asking God to give to us.

A few days after the banquet, still trying to discover
how I could make contact with the Rawlins family in
Salem, I called a friend in Salem who knew them and
asked him to initiate a meeting between us.

Imagine my surprise when a few days later my friend
called back and told me that he had just talked to
Dwayne Rawlins and he was the very man I had sat
beside at the banquet. My friend said that Dwayne was
eager to talk to me about the land.

In the six months of negotiations that followed,
Dwayne became the key person used of God to open up
minds and hearts of all the other people involved in the
negotiations.

How do you buy a million dollar property without any
money? Knowing that this was the property that
God wanted us to have, I became possessed with courage
and confidence. By myself I do not have that kind of

confidence. But as I discovered, *"I can do all things through Christ that strengtheneth me"* (Phil. 4:13, KJV). On July 19, 1979, unbelievable but true, we signed an earnest money agreement with very astute real estate investors to purchase this million dollar property without one dollar of money in our hand.

For anyone who knows the property, the people involved, and real estate dealings, the terms were unbelievable. Two of the parcels we would have on five-year options with fair annual payments to apply toward purchase. Later we were able to negotiate the purchase and release of a four-acre parcel we could own free and clear to build on.

Looking back on this miracle, I have to say that we got into this property the only way we could have—God's way. God has a way of making the impossible possible in your life.

Two weeks after signing the earnest money agreement, we ran into a big problem. Terrace Lawn Cemetery next door to the land that we were purchasing informed us that they had a long-standing option to buy two of the acres. The cemetery was small and in order to be a viable business, it was dependent upon getting these two acres. The plot thickened when we discovered that our seller did not want to sell the cemetery any land. Thus, we were right back in the middle of what threatened to become a knock-down, drag-out legal battle.

I entered into tedious, sometimes painful negotiations between the parties concerned. If you have ever been in the middle before, you know what I mean when I say it's not an easy place to be. This hassle went on for nine months. The hassle itself worked to our advantage in that it kept delaying the deadline for our $100,000 down payment, money that we did not have.

The last deadline was set for April 26, 1979. That was the day we had to come up with $100,000 or lose the opportunity of a lifetime to have the most choice spot upon which to build. Out of the sticky cemetery situation came our solution to the big $100,000 problem. An agreement was struck with the cemetery. They would pay us $90,000 cash for the two acres they needed. In turn we would pay the same $90,000 along with an additional $10,000 that our people had given in faith to make the $100,000 down payment. Once again what looked impossible became possible.

You never know what possibilities are contained within a problem.
With God's help turn all your problems into positive solutions.

MIRACLE DAY

Sunday, August 26, 1979, is the day that pioneers of New Hope's ministry will never forget. We put up a large tent on the miracle land at the exact spot that we planned to build our first church home. It was a hot day, but that didn't wither the spirit of expectation and enthusiasm as we gathered under the tent. In the morning's spectacular service, Margi sang prophetically "I Believe in Miracles." As she sang I looked out at the crowd of three or four hundred people and thought, *It's sure going to take a miracle today if we're going to raise the $250,000 we must have to build our miracle building.*

In the morning service I preached out of my heart with great vision and passion about what God wanted to use the ministry of New Hope to accomplish, and how we needed to give now to see this miracle building come into being. Although I gave it my best shot, the pledges in the morning weren't all that great. There followed one of the longest Sunday afternoons I have ever struggled through.

Fewer people were there in the evening, but something

happened that I'll never forget. People started sharing—
the older people, the little children, various ones
whose lives had been touched by New Hope. Saying yes
to the Spirit of God, they dug clear down and made
what looked like impossible commitments to give. As the
sun was going down, the board displaying 1,000 seats
at $250 each turned green and the people shouted and
praised God for the dream of having our own miracle
building.

IT LOOKS LIKE A DOVE

On September 14, 1979, the Sunnyside Road property we
had purchased but couldn't build on sold. A local
realtor interested in developing the property paid the
remaining balance on our contract and gave us a
note due in six months for $200,000 plus interest. In
three years God had taken the original $23,000 in seed
faith and multiplied it into $200,000. When the $200,000
is actually received, we will use it to purchase four
acres of our miracle land outright so that we can begin
construction of our first church home.

We could see it clear by then. Without having
purchased the Sunnyside Road property three years
before and without the subsequent profit from it, we
would have had no financial resources to purchase the
miracle land or begin construction on the miracle
building.

How much more perfect was God's plan than our plan!

GETTING UP AGAINST THE WALL

A few months later things are moving along nicely. The
architect will soon be finished with the plan. We have
committed ourselves to the builder to construct the

building. In believing faith people are giving their money, but now we are facing a big payment coming due.

In order to get the necessary portion of the land free and clear upon which to build, we must pay $130,000, due on January 7.

Interest rates are rising rapidly and hitting historic new heights. The purchaser of the Sunnyside Road property is running into difficulty and is unable to make even the interest payments on the money that is coming due us. What will we do, Lord? Where will the money come from? Have we come thus far by faith to lose this property now?

On January 7, the very day the money is due, a big storm hits the greater Portland area. All businesses are tied up. People are confined to their homes for the better part of a week. This ice storm delays the attorneys in getting the contract completed. We are given one more week to come up with the money.

I get on the telephone and start calling members of our New Hope family and asking them if they might be in a position to loan their church money on an unsecured note. Our state has a law that a church can take a limited number of such notes. On Tuesday, January 15, we are right at the limit. We can borrow on only one more note. The people have responded beautifully and we have $105,000. But we are still $25,000 short.

We have made arrangements with a local loan institution for the last $25,000. We are scheduled to pick up the money in the afternoon. So we postdate the check one day and our Business Manager, Jerry Schmidt, delivers the check for $130,000 to our attorney's office to meet the deadline.

But when Jerry goes to the loan office in the afternoon to pick up the check for $25,000, he gets the shock of his life.

As security for the loan we had agreed to put up our contract with the note receivable on the Sunnyside Road property. Earlier, when selling that property, we had signed legal documents that put us in a second position. But now an updated title report revealed that we had not been recorded in our rightful second position but in a third. And because we were recorded in a third position, the loan institution refused to loan us the $25,000. When Jerry phoned me with the bad news it made me sick in the pit of my stomach. That night was one of the most restless ones of my life.

God comes to our rescue!

The next morning one of my friends and parishioners, Ben Brantingham, introduced me to a business friend of his whom I had never met before. Within thirty minutes this man lent us the $25,000 on an unsecured note. People just do not do business that way. And yet this man did it. I believe that God did it through him.

Why should we worry and fret when God is in charge?

Such an experience produced a growing feeling that I am involved in something much bigger than I am. God has promised, *"I will build my church and the gates of hell shall not prevail against it"* (Matt. 16:18, KJV).

TEETERING BETWEEN SUCCESS AND FAILURE

I know what it is to fail. I know what it is to succeed. And I know what it is to teeter between success and failure.

In early January 1980, I was just beginning a long period of that kind of tense uncertainty. With interest rates hitting a historic high of 20 percent, we were unable to secure a large enough loan for the project. The loans from our people had enabled us to buy outright our building site, but those short-term notes were soon coming due and had to be repaid. But how?

During this period of heavy stress I had to fight off the fear of failure. My fear was not so much that I would personally fail. I had been that route before in my life and had survived. The deep fear I had was that I would let down thousands of people who had found new hope. Believe me, that is a heavy load to carry.

Through it all God had a recurring lesson that he wanted me to learn and to teach other people. What is that lesson which makes the difference between failure and success?

LEARNING TO LEAN

It's easy to trust God when things are rolling good. When everything is working out, who couldn't trust the Lord? But what about when nothing is turning out right? It seems to me that real trust is holding on however black the horizon. It's believing that God is at work when we don't see him at work.

In this period of my life I had to trust in the Lord. There was no other way of leading the New Hope people to accomplish something so far beyond us.

Trusting means believing.

One of my favorite Bible verses says, *"Trust in the Lord with all thine heart and lean not unto thine own under-standing"* (Prov. 3:5, KJV). These words from John Stallings' chorus, "Learning to Lean," have come to mean a great deal to me.

Learning to lean, learning to lean,
I'm learning to lean on Jesus.
Finding more power than I ever dreamed,
I'm learning to lean on Jesus.[1]

WHAT SHALL WE DO, LORD?

By April 1980, the plans for our miracle building were completed. The people were anxiously awaiting word that the project had begun. On a Thursday night that I will never forget, Gerald Bristol, the builder, called me and said, "I'm ready to start digging tomorrow. Shall we go or shall we wait?"

At that decision making moment the liabilities seemed great. We owed $130,000 in small notes to our people. They were coming due in thirty days, sixty days, ninety days. As hard as we had worked to secure a loan, we had yet to succeed. We had a halfway promise from a company in Texas that they would sell bonds for us, giving us two-thirds of the money we would need to complete the project. If they did do this, where would the rest of the money come from?

On the asset side we had a note receivable for $200,000 that everyday appeared more uncollectible.

What should we do? For days I had known that this moment of decision was coming. A banker, a Christian millionaire, and other financial advisors said, "Don't do it. It's too risky to build now." On the other hand we had already received our invitation to be out of Warner Pacific College as of January 1. The way the ministry was growing and the different need-meeting ministries multiplying, we desperately needed a home base.

It's marvelous how God prepares us ahead of time for important choices of our life. A few weeks before this decisive moment, a friend named Dean Eldridge, who lives in New Mexico, sent me a copy of Dr. Paul Cho's book, *The Fourth Dimension*. As I was wavering between doubt and faith, God used this book to build my faith.

Through the book my attention was focused again on the story of Moses standing at his decisive moment in front of the Red Sea. The crossing looked utterly impossible. From the ridge behind him came the distant thunder and flying dust raised by the approaching horses and chariots of Pharoah's army. They were coming down on top of the Israelites.

If ever there was an impossible situation, it was this one. The enemy closing in upon them. An angry uncrossable river in front of them.

Moses said, "What shall we do, Lord?" And then the Lord spoke to Moses and said, *"Speak unto the children of Israel, that they go forward"* (Ex. 14:15, KJV). On the very day before Gerald Bristol called me, I was asking the Lord, "What shall we do, Lord?" And he gave me his answer. It was the same word that he gave to Moses. He gave the word that we should get up and go forward. On that lonely night of heavy decision making, I told the builder, Gerald Bristol, "Let's go for it."

Make the right decision.
Then solve the problems.

WE ALMOST LOST IT ALL

The situation of the $200,000 plus interest due us from the sale of the Sunnyside Road property continued to deteriorate. The company that owed us the money had no means to pay it. As if that were not a big enough problem the man recorded wrongly ahead of us was foreclosing the property. This could mean we would lose it all. When a property is foreclosed, those recorded after the party doing the foreclosing are wiped out unless the bid is high enough to pay them also.

The doomsday sale was set for the last week in September of 1980 on the Clackamas County courthouse steps. I do not like to even think of what damage the loss of the $200,000 would have done to the already stretched project. It would have been curtains!

At the midnight hour on the courthouse steps the title company that had mistakenly recorded us in the third position came forward and protected us by purchasing the property themselves. Within hours they recorded us in our rightful position and three weeks later paid us the full $200,000 due on our note plus one year's interest.

The very mistake of being recorded in the lesser position that could have wiped us out is what God used to save us.

That glorious day when I picked up the payment in full from the title company I thought of the story of Joseph when he was revealing himself to his brothers and they were lamenting the mistake they had made toward him. They had done him an injury that could have wiped Joseph out. But Joseph declared that God took the mistake and brought a beautiful miracle out of it [Gen. 45:4-8].

What about it? Do you think it was a dove or a pigeon? I can tell you there is no doubt in my mind as to what kind of bird it was. It was God's sign of divine guidance.

Through these experiences and many more we have found that:

God leads his dear children along
Some through the water, some through the flood.
Some through the fire, but all through the blood.
Some through great sorrow, but God gives a song.
In the night season and all the day long.
[G. A. Young]

Last Sunday among the more than 2,000 people who attended our Sunday services I saw and greeted my friend, Wilma Travis. She and her husband, Walt, started attending New Hope just after we began our first drive-in services. Although Walt was well past retirement age, he caught the vision of what New Hope was all about. His faith came alive to an extent it never had before. Soon he and Wilma became our congenial greeters at the gate each Sunday morning, passing out the latest church publication.

Right in the midst of our struggles while we were trying
to obtain zoning and build on the Sunnyside Road
property, Walt became very ill and lay at the point of
death.

One of the last times I saw Walt alive, he said with
tears coming down his cheek, "Pastor, I so much wanted
to see the new church built." Then he began to sob
and said, "I'm not going to get to see it."

When the family went to look for a place to bury Walt,
they bought a cemetery lot on a lush green slope
right next door to where God has built his New Hope
Community Church. At the time they purchased the lot
for Walt's final resting place, none of us had any
idea of God's perfect plan for where his church would be
built.

This morning as I walked from my house to my office
in our miracle church building. I walked right past
where we laid Walt to rest. I have to believe that now Walt
sees the church that he longed to see. Yes, the New
Hope dream is something more than a dream. It has
become a reality.

[1]LEARNING TO LEAN by John Stallings, © Copyright 1976 by HeartWarming
Music. International copyright secured. All rights reserved. Used by
permission of The Benson Company, Inc., Nashville.

NEW HOPE—A REALITY!

I'm so glad I'm a part of the family of God. William J. Gaither

Aggie Hearst's parents were Swedish missionaries serving in the heart of undeveloped Africa. Aggie was only a few days old when her natural mother died. Her grieving father took the new baby and trudged many miles to an isolated mission station where he left her in the care of a missionary couple. A few months later all of the missionaries at that station died. Little baby Aggie was left in the care of native mothers who nursed her at their own breasts. When an American missionary couple arrived at the remote mission post, they found Aggie in the hands of native mothers and suffering from malnutrition.

The American couple quickly gave their hearts to the forlorn little baby. Intent on adopting Aggie, they returned home to America with their newfound bundle of joy. For a long time their efforts to contact her natural father were unsuccessful. When they finally did reach him, they asked permission to adopt Aggie. He replied that they could care for her and raise her but never would he surrender her for adoption.

The insurmountable problem was that without adoption Aggie could not become an American citizen. As a result Aggie was a woman without a country for the first forty years of her life. When I heard this story I thought, *It must be a terrible feeling to live in America and be deprived of belonging to the country.*

Several years ago a large city newspaper printed a human interest story titled, "He Would Like to Belong." The article told about a small boy who was riding on a downtown bus. There he sat, huddled close to an exquisitely dressed lady. When he rubbed his dirty shoes against the woman sitting on the other side of him, she said to the lady in the pretty dress, "Pardon me, but would you please make your little boy take his dirty feet off the seat?"

The well-dressed woman blushed. Then giving the little boy a shove, she said, "He's not my boy. I never saw him before."

Embarrassed, the lad put his head down and pulled his collar up as if to hide. He was such a small boy, with his feet dangling off the seat. It was obvious that he was fighting to hold back the tears.

"I'm sorry I got your dress dirty," he said to the woman. "I didn't mean to."

"It's all right," she answered, a little embarrassed. Then, since the little boy was still looking at her, she inquired, "Are you going somewhere alone?"

"Yes," he softly answered. "I always travel alone. I don't have anyone to go with me. You see, I don't have any mommie or daddy. They're both dead. I live with my Aunt Maggie, but she says Aunt Elizabeth ought to help take care of me part of the time. So when she gets tired of me and wants me to go someplace, she sends me over to stay with Aunt Elizabeth."

"Oh," said the woman. "Are you on your way to Aunt Elizabeth's now?"

"Yes," the boy continued. "But Aunt Elizabeth is hardly ever home. I sure hope she's home today, though, because it sure is cold."

The woman felt sympathy for this little guy and she said, "You're a very small boy to be riding the bus all by yourself."

He said, "It's OK. I never get lost but sometimes I do get awful lonesome. So when I see someone that I think I would like to belong to, I sit real close and snuggle up to them and pretend that they are my family. I was playing the 'I belong' game with the other lady when I got your dress dirty. I forgot about my feet."

The understanding woman put her arms around the little boy and held him close to her. He wanted to belong to someone. Deep down in her heart, she wished that he belonged to her.

The little boy who had no family expressed one of the deepest needs that we have in our lives. No matter how young you are or how old you are, there is that deep need to belong.

It is Christ's master plan for us to belong to each other. This is one of the reasons Jesus established the church, in order that we might belong to him and to each other. In a society in which so many have lost their family roots and are experiencing isolation and loneliness, the church is in a unique position to move into this vacuum and give people a loving, accepting, forgiving family in which to belong.

Back in the early 1970s when I was right in the middle of the crisis of losing my family, Bill Gaither released his new song entitled "The Family of God." I'll never forget one night when a singing group in the local church I was pastoring sang this song that speaks of belonging:

You have noticed we say brother and sister 'round here.
It's because we're a family and these folks are so near.
When one has a heartache we all shed a tear,
And rejoice in each victory in this family so dear.
I'm so glad I'm a part of the family of God;
I've been washed in the fountain, cleansed by His blood!
Joint heirs with Jesus as we travel this sod,
For I'm part of the family, the family of God.[1]

As the Gospel Folksingers sang this song, which has become a favorite of so many Christians around the world, the people present were blessed with the warm feeling of belonging to the family. I was sitting on the front row, and although the church was filled with people I felt more alone than I had ever felt in my entire life. At that moment I knew that because of my broken marriage I no longer really belonged to the church family I had known all my life. I was an orphan without a church.

For years I was to live with the hollow feeling of not belonging anymore to the church of my birth. You might say this was an ache but not a break. An ache in that it hurt, but not a break in that I refused to allow it to stop me from fulfilling the ministry to which God had called me. God had called me to reach out in love to the unchurched. And the amazing discovery that I made was that as I reached out to the unchurched in love, acceptance, and forgiveness, they responded and experienced the same transforming new hope that was changing my life. As the days, the months, and years went by, God gathered from the unchurched thousands his people into a local fellowship called New Hope Community Church.

In these ten years of adventurous ministry, thousands of hurting people who, for whatever reason, didn't belong anywhere, came and found that they did belong to Jesus and to each other.

Joe Schmidt, father of one of our staff pastors, Jerry Schmidt, attended one particular church most of his life for thirty years, but because he smoked, he was an outcast. There was always that underneath feeling— you're not one of us. Soon after we started New Hope, Joe and his family came. We immediately accepted him, loved him, and included him in the family. With this kind of love and acceptance, it wasn't long before Joe's faith came alive and he witnessed that now he belonged to Jesus. He became one of our faithful volunteers in the church office. His years spent at New Hope were the happiest years of his life. At his memorial service we celebrated his homegoing and sang together, *"I'm so glad I'm a part of the family of God."*

Everyone wants to belong. Because of my divorce and remarriage, there are circles within the evangelical church in which I am not accepted as a minister and maybe never will be. But I determined a long time ago that I could not let that stop me from fulfilling the call of God on my life to minister to the unchurched and now to the church that God has given to us. As I have been faithful to the ministry, God has given back to me a beautiful church family.

It was one of the most exciting days of our life, when on Sunday, February 9, 1980, Margi and I opened the doors of our own New Hope Community Church building. This was after having wandered from place to place for eight years, like the children of Israel in the wilderness. In each of the twelve locations we'd occupied during our journey, we kept visualizing our own dream church building and believing that it would become a reality. And now on this victory day our dream had come true. It was a good thing we had planned our first building to be a big one, because on opening Sunday our attendance jumped by 500 additional people and has been rapidly increasing every Sunday since.

Thursday night, March 11, 1981, was a memorable night of celebration when we dedicated our new church facility. The guest speaker for the occasion was internationally known television speaker, Dr. Robert Schuller. Fourteen hundred happy, expectant church family members and friends came to celebrate the magnificent dream come true. Sitting beside Dr. Schuller, with our wonderful full choir behind me, looking out over the family and seeing what God had done for us in these short years, was an exhilarating spiritual experience.

My wife, Margi, is my best friend and has been my partner every step of the way in the establishment of the great ministry of New Hope. When she stood that night and sang, like an angel, "How Great Thou Art," my emotion of joy overflowed. At that high and holy moment there came the witness deep within my soul that I belonged to the family of God. No longer was I to feel like an orphan without a church. I had a church family and I belonged!

God promised Joel the prophet that after disaster *"I will make up to you for the years that the swarming locust has eaten . . . and you shall have plenty to eat and be satisfied"* (Joel 2:25, 26, NASB). That promise has become my reality. Anything I have ever lost in my life, God has given back—and so much more. Believe this! Good things are going to flow once again into your life. Look to Jesus and believe—the best is yet to come!

New Hope is a dream come true.

What a personal satisfaction it has been for the New Hope family to occupy its own church building! Out of the eight years of wandering from place to place and not having our own church, one lesson has been engrained in us. This is a lesson that every church, to be

effective, must learn. What is this essential lesson?
It is that the church is not a building but a fellowship of
people. People needing people. People learning how
to receive God's love and to give it to each other. People
ministering to each other in Christ's name. People
working to help fulfill each other's dreams and healing
each other's hurts. Everyone needs to belong to such a
church.

Already at New Hope Community Church we have a
need-meeting Positive Christian Singles Group that
ministers to hundreds of people. We have a dynamic
youth ministry that is exciting to be around. We have
small groups in homes that we call our "Tender
Loving Care Groups" where people share and grow
together in close fellowship. We have a Positive Christian
Women's Fellowship that comes together every week
to lift and inspire women to be beautiful for Jesus. We
have an alcoholic-drug ministry that we call "Alcoholics
Victorious" to help people beat the drug and alcohol
problem. We have a strong family emphasis, with
seminars, classes, marriage retreats, and family camp to
help build strong Christian homes. We have a college
and career singles ministry to help those recently out of
high school through their important decision making
years. We have a host of men and women trained to work
as lay pastors in assisting the pastors in ministry.
We have a staff of five very unique, special pastors and
their wives, who love each other and work together
as a team. We have a prayer ministry that lifts daily
requests to the Lord and prays for the healing of the
hurting and sick. We have a professonal counseling
center headed by a trained psychologist with a doctor's
degree and years of experience. He does a tremendous
job of helping people who hurt. We have a book
ministry that reaches hundreds of thousands of people.
We have a large music program second to none in

the city. It inspires people to praise the Lord and celebrate living for him. We have a host of volunteers who work together to do the work of the Lord. My dream has become a reality! New Hope is something more than a dream!

At thirty-one, I saw a black curtain drop announcing the death of my ministry as a pastor. But because Jesus is alive I refused to give up hope. I kept believing that somehow, some way, if I was faithful to God, he would use my life again. At forty-three, I am having the best days of ministry I've ever had. I believe in miracles! Because my life and ministry are truly miracles of God.

It has been my personal experience that it is always the darkest just before the morning. But after the night, the morning does come. As the first rays of daylight break through the darkness, the miracle of a new day begins. This miracle happens not once but 365 times every year. The dawning of each new day reminds us again and again that *God specializes in new beginnings.*

God is not only there when the sun comes breaking through, but also when the night is the blackest. When I felt so alone, so scared and wiped out, he was there all the time.

No matter how bad things are, you are not without hope because God works not only in the daytime, but also in the nighttime of our lives. Faithfully, quietly, he works his perfect will, and like the skillful weaver, he brings something beautiful out of chaos.

God brings beauty out of ashes.

There have been times in my life when I was hurt so deeply that the will to die was stronger than the will to live. That is a terrible place to be. But I can joyfully witness that, even at that low point, God was still at work in my life. I have found the words of Romans 8:28 not only a wonderful promise, but also a reality:

*And we know that all things work together for good to them
that love God, to them who are the called according
to his purpose.*

God has taken everything, both good and bad, that has
happened in my life and used it to make me a better
person, a person he can use more effectively in loving
others.

What am I saying? I'm saying that even if you have
suffered a severe setback, life isn't over. The same God
who put the broken pieces of my life together, the
same God who is using my life today in greater ways than
ever before, the same God I've seen heal hurts and
rebuild the dreams of thousands is at work this moment
in your life. Look to Jesus Christ. Dare to dream a
new dream! Believe that with God's help your beautiful
dream can come true.

ELEVEN

MAKE LOVE YOUR NUMBER ONE AIM

Success is nothing unless you have someone you love to share it with.

What do you do when you have lost in love? Scores of people do what comes naturally. They pull back in their shell and hide. They say, "I'm never going to get hurt like that again." I understand those feelings. When my wife left me, that's exactly how I felt. But to hide brings no cure for the hurt. To hide means to go on hurting without ever being healed.

What can heal my hurt? Nothing can heal the spirit that has been wounded by the loss of love like experiencing love again. There is no emotional wounding that a person cannot recover from completely by learning to receive and give love again. Love is a miraculous healing medicine.

Back in 1970, like some of you who have lost in love, I had an enormous need for someone to love me and accept my love in return. Losing in love did not do away with my need for love, but it intensified and enlarged the need. Feeling all alone, I longed to feel close to someone. Having failed in love, I had the enormous need to succeed in love.

I believe it is God's will for us to love again. First of all because God is love, and love is his better way for us, his children, to live on this earth. And second, because it is not God's will for us to be failures. To the contrary, I believe God wants you and me to use even our failings as stepping stones to success.

When God first gave man birth and worth, he said, *"It is not good that the man should be alone; I will make him an help meet for him"* (Gen. 2:18, KJV). It didn't take me very long to discover that I lacked the gift of singleness. I understand there are a few people who do have this gift. Not me. All my life I had lived in a family. I loved to belong to a family. In order to be fulfilled and completed, I needed to belong to a family.

I believe that God, who knows me better than I know myself, brought into my life a very special person when he brought Margi and me together. Margi is a very warm person who initiates love in all of her relationships with others. God has used Margi to teach me many things about the beauty of love.

In his book *Love Life* (Grand Rapids: Zondervan Publishing Co., 1980), Ed Wheat teaches we can have five kinds of love. They are:

Romantic love
Sexual love
Belonging love
Friendship love
Agape love

Agape love is the purest, most perfect love there is. It comes into our lives through fellowship with the Divine One and flows out as an unselfish, unconditional love for others. I believe that Margi and I have a growing, fulfilling marriage because during our ten years of married life we have chosen and cultivated all five kinds of love in our marriage relationship.

Margi's beautiful love given to me has released me to be
a more outgoing, warm person in all of my relationships
with people. It has also given me the daily support
and confidence to tackle impossible things for God. In
addition, I've found our moments alone with each
other away from work and the crowds and responsibilities
to be priceless, warm times of oneness. Isn't that
what the Lord said marriage was all about? *"Therefore
shall a man leave his father and his mother; and
shall cleave unto his wife; and they shall be one flesh"*
(Gen. 2:24, KJV).

Love is something more than a fairy tale.

For me the love shared between a good and faithful
wife and a devoted husband has been the most fulfilling,
rewarding experience of life. But this kind of love
relationship doesn't just happen. It only happens when
two people make the commitment to learn to love
each other God's way.

The most important lesson for any married couple to
learn is one that I learned the hard way. I confess that a
failing in my first marriage, on my part, was that
although I loved my wife and my two children, in daily
practice I showed that I loved my work more. After
a long day of hard work, my family got what was left over
and most of the time that wasn't very much.

I mistakenly modeled my life after the ministers I knew
throughout my growing-up years. They taught me to
put the church first and family second. How wrong we
all were!

The Bible talks about three institutions ordained of
God: the family, the nation, and the church. A close
examination of Scripture reveals that the family is the first
and most important institution of God, and when it
fails all else crumbles.

There is no achievement without goal-setting. Goals

are critical to success, and of all the goals you might choose none is more important to a meaningful life than this one: *"Make love your number one aim"* [See 1 Cor. 14:1].

Today I have many goals that I intend, with God's help, to achieve in my lifetime. None is greater than this love goal, which has become my number-one aim in life.

How does this work out in everyday life? For me it means that my relationship with my wife has top priority in everything I do.

Success is nothing unless you have someone you love to share it with.

Allow me to illustrate. When our son, Scott, was born five years ago, I had a full week's schedule committed. Committee meetings, speaking engagements, something every night. In the beginning years of my ministry I would have missed the golden opportunity of sharing this time with my wife. I would have done the work of the church and felt guilty because I wasn't with my wife. But because I am now free and making love my number-one aim, I either cancelled every activity or had someone else do it for me. Each day that first week, I spent the whole evening sharing the joy of our little Scott with Margi. These were moments to remember.

A problem I see in so many marriages today is that couples do not take enough time away from pressures and daily routine to have fun and enjoy being together. Unless you plan time to be together, your love wears thin and after long neglect, dies. Margi and I plan regular times just to be together away from everything else, to have fun and enjoy being together. We work together, we sleep together, we pray together, and most of all, we get away from it all together.

The other day a group of ministers was coming through our building and they asked me this question,

"To what do you attribute the phenomenal growth and success of this church?" I shocked them, I think, when I answered, "LOVE." It's not the fantastic programs, though we've got some pretty amazing ones. The way to build a great church is to teach people by example how to love.

The most important thing in my life is the love relationship with Margi and my children. If that's not what it should be, then I drop everything else until it is straightened out. Unless you pay attention to love, it can die from indifference. Love can only grow and thrive when it's given your best. Next to my love relationship with my wife is my love relationship with my staff and their families. And then with the leaders and workers in our church.

Admittedly it is not always easy to love Christ's way. What do you do when someone has hurt you? If you're going to love Christ's way, you're going to forgive often when you don't feel like forgiving. You're going to be the initiator of healing, seeking reconciliation between yourself and that other person even when you haven't done anything wrong. God has called us to love each other his way—his superior way. There is nothing greater than love.

I am reminded of John the Apostle when he was growing old. Tradition tells us that this Son of Thunder who became known as the Apostle of Love, at the end of his life kept saying over and over these last words: *"Little children, come love one another. Little children, come love one another."*

Let me tell you that love has worked a miracle in my life. And love can work a beautiful miracle in your life. Believe it! God's love can heal all your hurts and make beautiful dreams come true in your life.

**Love is your greatest possibility!
There is no other!**

POSTSCRIPT

In each of the six previous books I have written, I have
had a special dedication page upon which I honored
someone who meant a lot to me personally. However, in
the front of this book you found no such dedication
page. Instead I have chosen to close this book with a
tribute to a special person without whom my dream
of New Hope would have never become a reality.
*Margaret Louise Watson Galloway, this is my tribute
to you.*

I love you because you are—Margi.
There is no one else just like you; you are special.
Blonde and beautiful.
Delightful and cheerful.
Inquisitive and expressive.
Unselfish and giving.
You are my girl!

I love you for sharing:
My hopes and dreams.

My successes and failures.
Our children.
The ministry of New Hope.
And I love you for all the memories.

I love you for being:
Loyal and true.
Honest and communicative.
Open and forgiving.
Special and serving.
Loving and responsive.

I love you for what you do for me.
You complete me.
You encourage me.
You complement me.
You inspire me.
You fulfill me.
You make me so much more than I could be without you.
You are my helpmate.

Margi, you are:
My daily delight.
My unfailing friend.
My Christian companion.
To me, the most beautiful girl in all the world.
My dearest Margi, I love you!